THE ETERNAL PROMISE

The Eternal Promise

by
Thomas Kelly

A Sequel to *A Testament of Devotion*

Friends United Press
Richmond, Indiana

Library of Congress Cataloging-in Publication Data

Kelly, Thomas R. (Thomas Raymond), 1893-1941.
    The eternal promise: a sequel to A testament of
devotion/by Thomas Kelly. — 2nd Friends United
        Press ed. p.   cm.
    Reprint. Originally published: New York:Harper &
    Row. 1966.
    Includes index.
    ISBN 0-944350-02-X
    1. Devotional literature. 2. Christian life — Quaker
    authors.
I. Title.
BV4832. K4297 1988
248.4'896—dc19   87-30383
                                                   CIP

Published by arrangement with Harper & Row

Harper & Row edition published in 1966
First Friends United Press edition 1977
Second Friends United Press edition 1988
Copyright 1966 Richard M. Kelly

Contents

Foreword

Although I have never met Thomas Kelly, he has become my friend. In the "Blessed Community" unbounded by time, geography, or creed, Kelly himself counted Francis of Assisi, Brother Lawrence, and John Woolman among his dearest friends, and, in the same way, over the last fifty years, thousands of men and women, I among them, have taken Tom Kelly as their friend. We have known each other in God.

Most of Kelly's sisters and brothers in the Holy Fellowship have known him only through *A Testament of Devotion*, a posthumous collection of essays and speeches which has become a devotional classic since its publication in 1941. Less well-known but equally powerful is this collection, *The Eternal Promise*, made twenty-five years later by his son, Richard Kelly. I welcome its republication, for in this splendid book I have continued my conversation with this friend. Now many others can share in it as well. Because these essays and talks come from the same period of Kelly's life and because they radiate the same glow from the fire burning in his heart, they deserve to be as widely known as *Testament*.

Though most of Kelly's writing and speaking was done in a Quaker context, his wide influence demonstrates that his witness to the life with God knew no sectarian boundaries. It touches the highest that we know and hope about life and about God.

One reason for Kelly's broad appeal lies in his understanding of the "seeker." He knows that many of us, both inside and outside of the church, long for something more than the "common, mild, gentle, half-hearted conventional religiosity" which we so often experience. We want authentic, vital, life-changing faith. He also knows that our dissatisfaction is born less of spiritual blindness than of a vision of something greater, a vision engendered by God's gracious Presence itself. "We are all seekers," he says, "for we feel that we are sought." But, most of all, Kelly assures us that what we long for is indeed possible. In doing so, he gives us witness rather than argument, description rather than definition.

Kelly's exuberant witness is breath-taking. Everywhere we encounter words like "miraculous," "amazing," "astonishing," "triumphant," and "radiant." In a time when such words have been cheapened by their misuse, we hardly know whether to trust them. Yet when Kelly talks of "an astounding, an almost miraculous Life," we not only want to believe it, we also sense that this is not just talk, but experience.

It persuades and even amuses me that Kelly balks at his own extravagance. He would rather be more tempered, more sophisticated, more believable, but he knows that would betray the truth of his experience. At one point, he hesitates slightly, "...if it didn't sound silly to say it." Elsewhere we see this teacher of philosophy from a fine Eastern college saying, "I know I'm talking like an old-time evangelist. But I can't help that, nor dare I restrain myself and get prim and conventional. We have too long been prim and restrained. The fires of the love of God, of our love toward God, and of His love toward us, are very hot." As I feel what must be an almost blushing boldness, I know it must be true. As helpless as Amos, Jeremiah, or John, he must tell of what he has seen and tasted and handled; he must tell, simply and directly, what he knows by heart.

Like the old-time evangelist, Kelly goes beyond witness to invitation. He tells us that the life of wonder for which we long is not just for courageous prophets and cloistered saints. It is possible for everyone. It is a life known by "housewives and hand workers, plumbers and teachers, learned and unlettered, black and white, poor and perchance even rich." And Kelly invites us to experience it for ourselves. "Begin now," he says. Do you want to live such a life? "If you do, then you can." "...You may wistfully long for it; it can be yours." "Hasten unto God," he urges. "There you will find rest for your souls, and power, and peace, and joy unspeakable and full of Glory." It is a call which appeals powerfully to our deepest yearnings.

The Eternal Promise, like *A Testament of Devotion*, collects a variety of small pieces, each of which is valuable by itself. "The Gathered Meeting," for example, is one of the most useful discussions of worship that I know, with implications reaching well beyond the bounds of Friends tradition. "The Quaker Discovery" transcends doctrine to call us to "a rediscovery of the life and power and fellowship and joy and radiance which moved the early Church." And "Hasten unto God" is an extraordinarily moving and insightful call to discipleship. Yet through the individual pieces run some persistent themes which shape them all and give them the unique stamp of Thomas Kelly.

The heart of Kelly's thought is his conviction that God is here among us, pursuing us and wooing us. "The basic condition [for spiritual awakening]," he writes, "is the soul-shaking discovery that God himself is active, is dynamic, is here, is brooding over us all, is prompting and instructing us within, in amazing immediacy." It is a simple but liberating truth. Many people, thinking God distant from their world, can scarcely imagine they can meet and converse with God in the same way as the prophets and apostles did. To discover that they can throws open a whole new way of life.

For Kelly, however, the reality of God's Presence was not primarily something to believe, but something to experience. As a teacher of philosophy Tom Kelly knew well the classical arguments for God, but he objected that they left him cold, and he often warned of the dangers of mere religious learnedness. What mattered to Kelly was knowing God first-hand and not by hearsay, personally and not just out of books.

Some years before his own spiritual renewal Kelly wrote from Germany about becoming comfortable with the German language. "Knowing a language through the ear and tongue," he noted, "is vastly different from recognizing the meaning of written sentences." That observation describes Kelly's own spiritual growth as well. Language about God becomes vivid and authentic only when we are immersed in this Life and Presence. Beyond and prior to creeds and orthodoxies, "the center of religion is in a living, vital, unspeakably intimate fellowship of the soul with God, wherein we sing and dance and leap for joy in His Presence."

About the way to this life with God, Kelly is equally clear. It is the way of complete surrender. The "totalitarian claims of the gospel" will brook no half-heartedness, no mild devotion. It requires that we follow our God-hunger to the "point of utter exhaustion," and that we throw caution to the wind. He writes, "Fearing excess we have not feared caution," and adds elsewhere: "Better to run the possible risk of fanaticism by complete dedication to God than to run the certain risk of mediocrity by twenty-percent dedication." Unrestrained devotion. Complete submission. That these must be our path is a central paradox of faith. We must lose to gain, must die to self to rise to a new life in God.

Kelly writes often and compellingly of this new life in a divine Center. It is a life of wholeness and integration in which we finally become our full selves. It is a life of "unhurried assurance" and peace and "amazing quiet power" in the midst of all the clamor about us. It is a life lived out of this divine Center, an inward sanctuary which Kelly variously calls a "Holy Place," the "Holy of Holies," "the Inward Glory," and, recalling a Hebrew term for God's dwelling Presence, "The Shekinah of the Soul." It is a cloister in the heart which empowers us to live extraordinary lives in the ordinary world.

Part of Kelly's appeal is that he insists on the possibility of glory in everyday life. He refuses to divorce the spiritual from the social and practical. So we live on two levels at once — the inner dialogue with God and the outer round of our daily tasks. We learn to love the world because God loves the world through us. And in doing so, we are led to varieties of service and almost certainly to suffering, not as a means to an end, but as the natural harvest of our life in God. In Kelly's words, "To give the message we must be the message."

Just as Kelly knows that this authentic life does not withdraw us from the world, he also knows that it does not separate us from our companions in faith. Private religion alone will not do. Indeed, as we come to know God in the Center, we discover that we are part of the "communion of saints," the "Holy Fellowship," the "Blessed Community," both historic and contemporary. We are knit together in the Eternal, often with people we least expect. This community of faith cuts across lines of public visibility and theological respectability, for it is not an organization, but simply a fellowship of those who know God first-hand.

BLINDED BY SPLENDOR

Virtually all *The Eternal Promise* and *A Testament of Devotion* come from the last three years of Kelly's life, beginning in early 1938. During that winter people around Kelly began to comment on the change they saw in him as these speeches and essays erupted from a new fire within. Yet since change rarely occurs in a vacuum, we must wonder what nurtured and precipitated the high vision and the luminous words which still search our hearts.

Clearly Kelly's life is not a gutter-to-glory story. He had a long history of personal preparation and devotion — study, worship, public ministry, and service — before this new surge of life overtook him. In a sense, like Paul he was a Pharisee of Pharisees. And, like Paul, his gifts with words and ideas proved to be powerful resources to describe the new life he had found. Yet, also like Paul, who counted his heritage and achievement as so much rubbish, Kelly came to discount his impressive background. "Blinded by the splendor of God," he underwent a marked and abrupt change.

The precipitating crisis of this change, what T. Canby Jones has called a "second conversion," was a crushing personal defeat. Though Tom Kelly had a Ph.D. in philosophy from Hartford Theological Seminary and was teaching at prestigious Haverford College, he still longed for the kind of recognition that a Harvard Ph.D. would grant him. So he pursued this second doctorate, at great cost both physically and financially, completing all of its requirements except the final oral exams. When he stood for his orals in the fall of 1937, his mind went completely blank in a "woozy spell," a dreadful reprise of an earlier experience at Hartford, and he failed the exams miserably. For Kelly, to be denied the degree was catastrophic and it drove him to deep depression. Yet within months, out of the ruins of this dream rose a new, capturing vision.

The new life that had visibly sprouted in early 1938 quickly grew to maturity and harvest, partly through suffering and partly through the rich fellowship of the timeless "communion of saints."

In Hitler's Germany in the summer of 1938, Kelly was shaped by the suffering of others. "I have never had such a soul-overturning summer or period as this," he wrote. "It is not merely heroism, it is depth of consecration, simplicity of faith, beauty in the midst of poverty or suffering, that shames us. I have met some giant souls.... one can't be the same again." In this summer Kelly says he also learned "the real pain of suffering *with* people." Compassion as suffering with people is a theme developed later in Abraham Heschel's remarkable book *The Prophets*, and it is striking to see that Heschel and Kelly share a common root. Indeed, we know from Kelly's correspondence that Heschel was the young rabbi whom Kelly met in 1938 and about whose fate he wonders in "Where Are the Springs of Hope?" Through these short months in Germany, then, Kelly was quickly deepened by seeing and sharing the sufferings of others.

Tom Kelly grew to a new maturity also by sinking deep roots in the devotional classics. Certainly he had known them from seminary days and from his colleague Rufus Jones, who exposed him to Meister Eckhart and other medieval mystics. Yet now having entered the "Holy Fellowship" more fully, he found them "illuminated" and discovered that they nurtured "the flaming vision of the wonder of such a life." His sense of fellowship with them was so great that apart from Jesus, he said, Brother Lawrence (*The Practice of the Presence of God*), Francis of Assisi (*Little Flowers*), and John Woolman (*Journal*) were his "three dearest spiritual friends and patterns." Beyond these, however, he kept company with many others such as Augustine (*Confessions*), Jacob Boehme, Meister Eckhart, Thomas a Kempis (*The Imitation of Christ*), Jean Nicholas Grou (*Spiritual Maxims and How to Pray*), George Fox (*Journal*), and with some of his contemporaries like Evelyn Underhill and Frank Laubach (*Letters by a Modern Mystic*). It can be a remarkable and enticing fellowship for us all. At times our sense of kinship can be very strong as we say, often with relief, "At last, here is someone who knows what my experience is like." At other times these dear friends can guide us into paths we have not yet discovered. At all times, for those who can receive it, immersing ourselves in the classics is much more than reading great, old books. It is conversing with companions in the life with God.

Thomas Kelly was forty-four years old when his "breakthrough," as Meister Eckhart might have called it, took place. I have wondered whether the new life we see in him came partly out of struggling with personal and spiritual tensions common in mid-life and whether the disappointment at Harvard was the catalyst for a dramatic resolution of those tensions. Even if it were not appropriate to suggest that Kelly was going through a "midlife crisis," as we now call it, certainly several new dimensions in his experience reveal an energizing resolution to common midlife themes.

The most obvious change is in his coming to a profound sense of yieldedness. It is the "degree of holy and complete obedience and of joyful self-renunciation" in which "difference of degree passes over into utter difference of kind." This yielding to God's work is one in which we are less willful in our spiritual lives and we become open and receptive rather than controlling and manipulative. And we see, as Kelly did so clearly, that God has been at work all along. In our seeking, we discover we have been found. Our yieldedness goes hand in hand with a sense of trust, a settledness, a deep sense of grounding in God as our Home, our Refuge, the one who undergirds us with the Everlasting Arms.

Other dimensions of Kelly's growth also flow out of this radical "disowning" of ourselves in "holy obedience." There is growth in patience and in the strength to endure the dark night of the soul. "Give us of Thy cosmic patience," Kelly prays. "Blind us to discouragement and to anxious fears." There is a new integration of life and "a wholly new evaluation of outward things" in which we are "blind to the petty valuations of the world." And there is, most gloriously for Kelly, peace. Kelly captures the change in this challenge: "Serene, unhurried, undismayed, miraculous lives can be lived by you and by me, if we continuously will away the last vestige of claim upon ourselves and become wholly God-enthralled."

To my delight, this new edition of *The Eternal Promise* includes two additional selections, one of which has not been published before. "The Children of the Light," written the weekend before Kelly's sudden death, has been available only in *Thomas Kelly: A Biography* (Harper & Row, 1966). The other selection, "Have You Ever Seen a Miracle?" has been read only by those fortunate enough to get a mimeographed copy. In my judgment, this address given to seminarians in early 1940 shares the compelling beauty and insight of Kelly's better-known

15

writings and deserves the wider readership it can now have.

Some readers will note that in re-issuing this volume we have not revised Kelly's language to make it conform readily to current concerns about inclusive language. We have chosen, instead, to be faithful to Kelly's own prose and era, though I have no doubt that were Kelly our contemporary, he would be sensitive to this issue. Indeed, in his essay "Room for the Infinite" he speaks of how "we feel our way back to the world's Mother, as the child feels its way to its parent's arms," an expression more in tune with 1987 than 1937.

Finally, for those who love *A Testament of Devotion*, I hope that this will become an indispensable companion volume. For those who have not yet met Tom Kelly, I hope he will soon become their dear friend. But, most of all, I hope that these pages can allow Kelly to continue to do what he regarded as "the most fundamental thing anyone can do" — to bring people into the presence of God and leave them there.

Howard Macy
Wichita, Kansas
Fall, 1987

Editor's Preface

The interior life of spiritual discovery is not a rare or unusual occurrence. It is found in all generations and in all circumstances of life. Many embrace it with every fiber of their being, becoming uplifted, transformed, remade in the likeness of their vision. Most of us, however, find ourselves glimpsing such a life from afar. We can hardly believe that it might be ours; or rather, that we, you and I, are called to such a life; that we could be swallowed in the Ocean of Light and Love that is within us. And we comfort ourselves with the thought that this is stuff of sainthood and genius. But it is not. It is the stuff of everyday life if we be willing to open ourselves and give ourselves unreservedly to it.

Thomas Raymond Kelly wrote of this life. But his uniqueness does not lie in the depth of his own vision, though there is no question that he did go deeply into the mystical abyss. Rather, his uniqueness lies in his ability to communicate the vision through the written and spoken word. The continuing sales of *A Testament of Devotion* attest to the writer's extraordinary power to share his interior life with us. During the twenty-five years since its posthumous publication, *A*

17

Testament of Devotion has come to be recognized as a classic of devotional literature.

At the time of its publication no one suspected that such would be the case. Thomas Kelly died in January, 1941, leaving a literary legacy which amounted to a smattering of essays and lectures written primarily within the last three years of his life. At best they are only a prelude to what might have been had he lived and continued to write. In these three years, however, the quality of his writings is remarkable. Though the experience of which he wrote was relatively new to him, he was already an accomplished writer, bringing years of scholarly writing and teaching to the task of expressing the spiritual upheaval that came to him in the winter of 1937-1938. A sample of this earlier writing will be found in *Thomas Kelly — A Biography.*

His outlook and understanding continued to grow in those three years as the nature of the God-directed life became clear to him. One has only to compare "The Eternal Now and Social Concerns," from *A Testament of Devotion,* which was written within a few weeks of his initial "openings," with "The Gathered Meeting," from this volume, which was written in 1940, to see how this insight had deepened.

A Testament of Devotion was compiled after Thomas Kelly's death by Douglas Steere, who included the five most obvious essays. The current book includes the bulk of the remaining material which was written during that most crea-

*Harper & Row, 1966.

tive period. Two articles of an earlier date are also included. A number of letters are also available to the reader in *Thomas Kelly — A Biography*.

The general part headings which I have given are somewhat arbitrary though an effort has been made to provide groupings by subject matter. Neither this volume, nor its predecessor, presents its material in chronological order. For those who are interested, the following chronology is suggested. Unfortunately, an exact dating of all manuscripts is not possible.

American Christianity: 1926-1928.
Room for the Infinite: 1936 (published in 1937).
Quakers and Symbolism: early 1938.
The Eternal Now and Social Concern: early 1938.
Richard Cary Lecture: summer, 1938.
Hasten unto God: fall, 1938.
The Simplification of Life: early 1939.
Holy Obedience: spring, 1939.
Religion for this Distraught World: April, 1939.
Where Are the Springs of Hope?: summer, 1939.
The Blessed Community: summer, 1939.
Reflections: summer, 1939.
The Quaker Discovery: fall, 1939.
The Publishers of Truth: March, 1940.
Secret Seekers: summer, 1940.
Christians and Decided Christians: fall, 1940.
The Gathered Meeting: fall, 1940.
Reality of the Spiritual World: winter, 1940.
The Light Within: January, 1941.

Appreciation is expressed to the publishers of the various periodicals who have given permission to reprint many of the articles included here. Specific acknowledgement of the source is given at the beginning of each section.

Of his own writing Thomas Kelly says: "...descriptions themselves are always fragmentary substitutes: immediacy is their goal and true replacement. Therefore these words are not meant to be merely intellectual, static word pictures; a burning urge toward completion in immediacy underlies them. May these words and this speaker step aside, having sowed their mission, and the Life and the Light itself be your guide."

Thus is the Eternal Promise.

Richard M. Kelly
Brightwater, Maine
August, 1965

PART ONE

Religion for this Distraught World

This part contains four sections. The first, "American Christianity," was written about 1927. It is strikingly similar in emphasis to his later writings. "Christians and Decided Christians" was originally published in the Friends Intelligencer, *November, 1940. The third section is a collection of excerpts from the Richard Cary Lecture of 1938. This lecture was an enlargment of "The Eternal Now and Social Concern." Those portions which represent a duplication have been removed. No attempt has been made by the editor to create a continuous piece from the residual. The title article comes from an address to Quakers in Cleveland, Ohio, and was later published in the* American Friend, *1939. The final article in this part, "Where are the Springs of Hope?" is from a manuscript published posthumously in* Motive.

I

American Christianity

I visited recently in Holland a Dutch friend who had spent two years in America in an Eastern theological seminary. He was back in his homeland, a minister in a small city near Zuyder Zee. He said, "I am glad for the years I had in America. I learned much there about boys' work, and church activities, and social clubs, that is valuable to me here. I heard ministers, when the Japanese Exclusion Act was passed, cry out against it in their pulpits, declaring it to be unchristianlike or unchristian, and I appreciated it. But my people here, when they meet me, are hungry to know about God. They want to talk about the problems of religious faith. They want to understand how the Love of God is related to His forgiveness of sins, and how a Being outside of time can be known by beings in time. And in the church they are not anxious for a social message, but they want to be lifted into the Presence of the Ineffable One, caught up into the third heaven where they hear unspeakable words which it is not lawful for man to utter."

The favorite answer, or the Anglo-Saxon answer, to those whose interest is in the transcendent mysteries is, "Why stand ye gazing up into heaven while a hungry world surrounds you?" We take delight in reminding them that the smoking embers of an unholy war lie about their places of prayer, likely to flicker again into flame if they turn not their eyes from heaven to the need of this world for a practically-demonstrated reincarnation of Christ in daily ordering of affairs. We agree that God's hand is strong to save, but we insist that this will happen only through the hand of man, who must *live* his religion in daily life.

But, while we glibly refute those who stand gazing into the Great Beyond, too many of us have failed to gaze into heaven more than a minute or two at a time because we have to hustle out to the garage and get the car in order to attend a special meeting on Christ and the Political situation, a very important meeting because, in a few weeks, the city manager form of government is coming up for vote and good Christians must be prepared to take their part.

But each needs the other's view; each needs to fill out his weakness with the other's strength. Certainly if the social implications of Christ's way have not become widely clear to those whose thoughts have loved to linger with God, we pray for fuller interpretation of the heavenly vision of the earthly round. But, as certainly, if we have become strong in world-betterment and in discernment of the modes of feeding the hungry and clothing the naked and supplying the cup of cold water to His little ones, we need to root these things more deeply in the heavenly vision of divine vistas of the meadows of God. Of each it is true, "These we ought to have done and not to have left the other undone."

The straightest road to social gospel runs through profound mystical experience. The paradox of true mysticism is that individual experience leads to social passion, that the nonuseful engenders the greatest utility. If we seek a social gospel, we must find it most deeply rooted in the mystic way. Love of God and love of neighbor are not two commandments, but one. It is the highest experience of the mystic, when the soul of man is known to be one with God himself, that utility drops off and flutters away, useless, to earth, that worldshaking conscious-ness of mankind in need arises in one and he knows himself to be the channel of Divine Life. The birth of true mysticism brings with it the birthday of the widest social gospel. "American" Christianity is in need of its deeper strain of expression of direct contact with God, as the source, not of world-flight, but of the most intensely "practical" Christianity that has yet been known.

II

Christians and
Decided Christians

Anyone who has lived in totalitarian Europe in recent years knows the intensity with which Nazi and Fascist and Communist converts fling themselves into the proclamation of their new gospels. No flaccid, conveniently conventional Christian has a message today for such impassioned converts to secular gospels. Only a decided Christian can hope to proclaim a significant gospel in these days.

This decidedness in a Christian is not to be confused with the decidedness of the bigot, or the man with a one-string gospel. It is not a decidedness about a particular doctrine. Such "decided" Christians are plentiful, but they are not the answer to the world's need. True decidedness is not of doctrine, but of life orientation. It is a commitment of life, thoroughly, wholly, in every department and without reserve, to the Inner Guide. It is not a tense and reluctant decidedness, an hysterical assertiveness. It is a joyful and quiet displacement of life from its old center in the self, and a glad and irrevocable replacement of the whole of life in a new and divine Center. It is a life lived out from an all-embracing center of motivation, which in glad readiness wills to do the will of the Father, so far as that will can be discerned. It is a life of integration, of peace, of final coordination of all one's powers, within a singleness of commitment. It is the final elimination of all *tolerated* double-mindedness, and the discovery of the power which comes from being "in the unity."

Such decidedness is not forced upon us by external circumstances. It cannot be whipped up as an artificial intensity, for the purpose of opposing the secular gospels of our day. It is of the essence of Christianity to be totalitarian in its claims. If we as Christians hope to be instruments of the Divine Life in these days, we must be ready to pass out of the stage of mere Christianity, to the stage of decided Christians.

This same demand for a decided Christianity is stirring all about us. Why are so many unchurched? It is not all due to apathy. It is not due wholly to Mammon worship, snug, smug, and convenient as such answers are. Is it not partly due to a desperate honesty, to a deep sincerity? Men and women everywhere — I find it especially true of college men — have a deep, deep demand within them for an absolutely vital religion, for an absolute ground and validation of life. This Inner Witness within them is sharper than a two-edged sword. It cuts through shams. It rejects confused and shilly-shally faiths. It is the *aqua-regia* which exposes and dissolves away all surface hypocrisies that have tried to pass as pure gold. Too many churches and church programs and church worships are elusive, archaic, watered down. The Inner Witness within our critical generation leads it to feel, often inarticulately, that *this* is not the answer to its soul's demand. No doubt many churches are visited and too hastily dismissed by overcritical, impatient persons. No doubt many critics are easily moved by pride of intellect, and are not yet humbled sufficiently to discover their souls' good in lowly form. However, the fact remains that the decided Christianity is what is sought, and where it is not found the inquirer wanders away, and all too often abandons his dream of finding the "Friend behind the Phenomena."

It is just this Inner Witness that has made men critical of halfhearted religions to which we can appeal. Here is a real point of entrance. Some criticism is largely rooted in intellectual snobbery, some criticisms are rationalizations. But, after discount is made of all these evasions, there is a core of sincerity in all men, a yearning for the Real, a deep-set hunger for the Homeland of the soul. They "fly as a cloud, as doves to their windows." The world is full of seekers, as it was in the days of the First Publishers of Truth. They are not sentimental, ostentatious seekers, but baffled, confused, hardheaded, discouraged seekers, yet seekers nonetheless. Some of them explain that they have grown up in postwar days and belong to the Lost Generation. But they seek, and criticize, and reject because they have felt the touchstone of Reality within themselves.

27

Already the Hound of Heaven has been baying on their track. They ask for a decided Christian faith. They own it when they find it. They are much too honest to claim it as their own unless they truly possess it. But they already possess a key of promise greater than they know.

The decided Christian may serve as the agent of the Spirit to bring other wavering persons to a like decisiveness. And only he can hope to point needy but seeking men to their true vocation as children of Truth.

III

Excerpts from the Richard Cary Lecture

There is an amazing, glorious, triumphant and miraculous victorious way of life of which I would speak. It lies beyond struggle and strain. The deeper anxieties it knows not; its soul is in effortlessness and peace, and yet also in infinite labor and strength, and victory is ever before it. Inward, it touches the periphery of the outward with exquisite techniques; outward, it brings all time and existence into the inner presence of the Divine Life, and refines the gold from the dross. In lowliness it is powerful. In unhurried assurance it bestrides this toppling world, and smiles patiently as it works. You who have found this Life — or have been found by it — know what I mean. To you [who], at first hand, experience and live in the life-center, no more words are necessary — we understand each other already. To you who may not know vividly such a life I hesitantly, yet also boldly, offer a description, not an argument. For a description rests primarily upon experience while an argument from postulates. For, like the Apostles, we are meant to be *witnesses* of that which we have seen and our hands have handled of the word of Life. Mystical religion is everywhere grounded in the experimental base.

But descriptions themselves are always fragmentary substitutes: immediacy is their goal and true replacement. Therefore these words are not meant to be merely intellectual, static word-pictures; a burning urge toward completion in immediacy underlies them. May these words and this speaker step aside, having sowed their mission, and the Life and Light itself be your guide.

...The Quaker discovery and message has always been that God still lives and moves, works and guides, in vivid immediacy, within the hearts of men. For revelation is not static and complete, like a book, but dynamic and enlarging, as springing from a *Life* and Soul of all things. This Light and Life is in all men, ready to sweep us into its floods, illumine us with its blinding, or with its gentle guiding radiance, send us tendered but strong into the world of need and pain and blindness. Surrender of self to that indwelling Life is entrance upon an astounding, an almost miraculous Life. It is to have that mind in you which was also in Jesus Christ. "Behold, I stand at the door and knock." In the silence of your hearts hear Him knock. Outward teachers can only lead us to the threshold. But "God Himself has come to lead His people." Such men and women must be raised up, heaven-led souls who are not "seekers" alone, but "finders," finders who have been *found* by the Father of all the world's prodigals.

....How different is the experience of Life... when the Eternal Presence suffuses it! Suddenly, unexpectedly, the Divine Presence is upon us. Secretly, astonishingly, we are lifted in a plateau of peace. The dinning clamor of daily events — so real, so urgent they have been! — is framed in a new frame, is seen from a new perspective. The former things are passed away; behold, they have become new. This world, our world, and its problems, does not disappear nor lose its value. It reappears in a new light, upheld in a new and amazing *quiet* power. Calm replaces strain, peace replaces anxiety. Assurance, relaxation, and integration of life set in. With hushed breath we do our tasks. Reverently we live in the presence of the Holy... Life itself becomes a sacrament wherein sin is blasphemy. A deep longing for personal righteousness and purity sets in. Old tempting weaknesses no longer appeal as they did before. In patience we smile in loving concern for those who rush about with excited desperation. Oh, why can they not see the ocean of light and love which flows completely over the ocean of darkness and death! But all things [are] in His Providence. A little taste of Cosmic Patience, which a Father-heart must have for a wayward world, becomes ours. The world's work is to be done. But it doesn't have to be *finished* by us. We have taken ourselves too seriously. The life of God overarches *all* lifetimes....

...In the experience of Presence each successive Moment of living is seen as a completion of the whole of Life's meaning. And that completed moment enters again into the next moment with its uniqueness and its novelty, and new synthesis and completedness are achieved. Time, as sheer flow, is tantalizing, torturing, tragedy. Time as experienced in its matrix and seedbed, the Eternal, is perpetual completion, triumph, release. Time as ever-stretched toward goals is endless disappointment and postponements; Time as continuously given within and flowing from the Eternal is charged with serenity and satisfaction. Were earthly life to end in *this* moment, all would be well. For this Here, this Now, is not a mathematical point in the stream of Time; it is swollen with Eternity, it is the dwelling place of God Himself. We ask no more; we are at home. Thou who hast made us for Thyself dost in each moment give us our rest in Thee. Each moment has a Before and After; but still deeper, it has Eternity, and we have tasted it and are satisfied. As the English poet Coleridge says: "We on honeydew have fed, and drunk the milk of Paradise." Would that I could put into words that complete readiness and completedness of each moment of life have intrinsic value. The profound satisfaction within it seems to come not from the earthly past, for that may have been stupid, nor from the earthly future, for that may seem dark. It seems to come from the deep springs of Eternal Life breaking into Time itself, nay, begetting Time itself, disclosing itself as the Alpha and Omega of time, and into the ears of its time-born children whispering the secret of eternal peace.

The experience is of an invasion from beyond, of an Other who in gentle power breaks in upon our littleness and in tender expansiveness makes room for Himself. Had we thought Him an intruder? Nay, His first odor is sweetness, His touch an imparting of power. Suddenly, a tender giant walks by our side, no, strides within our puny footsteps. We are no longer our little selves. As two bodies closely fastened together and whirled in the air revolve in part about the heavier body, so life gets a new center, from which we are *moved.* It is as if the center of life had been shifted beyond ourselves, so that we are no longer our old selves. Paul speaks truly when he says that we are no longer live, but Christ lives in us, dynamic, energetic, creative, persuasive. In hushed amazement at this majestic Other, our little self grows still and listens for whispers — oh some so faint — and yields itself like a little child to its true Father-guidance. Yes, the sheep knows its shepherd, in these holy moments of eternity.

The old self, the little self — how weak it is, and how absurdly confident and how absurdly timid it has been! How jealously we guard its strange precious pride! Famished for superiority-feeling, as Alfred Adler pointed out, its defeats must be offset by a dole of petty victories. In religious matters we still thought that we should struggle to present to God a suitable offering of service. We planned, we prayed, we suffered, we carried the burden. The *we*, the self, how subtly it intrudes itself into religion! And then steals in, so sweetly, so all-replacing, the sense of Presence, the sense of Other, and He plans, and He bears the burdens, and we are a new creature. Prayer becomes not hysterical cries to a distant God, but gentle upliftings and faint whispers, in which it is not easy to say *who* is speaking, we, or an Other through us. Perhaps we can only say: Praying is taking place. Power *flows* through us, from the Eternal into the rivulets of Time. Amazed, yet *not* amazed, we stride the stride of the tender giant who dwells within us, and wonders are performed. Active as never before, one lives in the passive voice, alert to be used, fearful of nothing, patient to stand and wait.

It is an amazing discovery, at first, to find that a creative power and Life is at work in the world. God is no longer the object of a belief; He is a Reality, who has continued, within us, His real Presence in the world. God is aggressive. He is an intruder, a lofty lowly conqueror on whom we had counted too little, because we had counted on ourselves. Too long have we supposed that we must carry the banner of religion, that it was *our* concern. But religion is not our concern; it is God's concern. Our task is to call men to "be still, and know that I am God," to hearken to that of God within them, to invite, to unclasp the clenched fists of self-resolution, to be pliant in His firm guidance, sensitive to the inflections of the inner voice.

For there is a life beyond earnestness to be found. It is the life rooted and grounded in the Presence, the Life which has *been found* by the Almighty. Seek it, seek it. Yet it lies beyond seeking. It arises in *being found.* To have come only as far as religious determination is only to have stood in the vestibule. But our confidence in our shrewdness, in our education, in our talents, in some aspect or other of our self-assured self, is our own undoing. So earnestly busy with anxious, fevered efforts for the Kingdom of God have we been, that we failed to hear the knock upon the door, and to know that our chief task is to open that door and be entered by the Divine Life.

There is an old, old story that the gateway to deep religion is self-surrender. Dr. Coomaraswamy, writing upon the art of India, says that all developed religions have as their center the experience of becoming unselfed. But falling in love is an old, old story in the history of the world, yet new to each individual when first it comes. Descriptions of the unselfing which comes with the Invading Love are no substitute for the immediacy of the experience of being unselfed by the Eternal Captain of our souls. Nor is there a freedom so joyous as the enslaving bonds of such amazing, persuading Love.

But according to our Christian conception of the unselfing in religion, to become unselfed is to become truly integrated as a richer self. The little, time-worn self about which we fretted — how narrow its boundaries, how unstable its base, how strained its structure. But the experience of discovering that life is rooted and grounded in the *actual*, active, loving Eternal One is also to experience our own personal life firm-textured and stable. For we are no longer imprisoned between birth and death, between yesterday and tomorrow, but Eternity is our home, while our daily affairs are coordinated in that supernal light. Profound immersion in the Divine Love is a shaking experience. But it is not an unsettling experience; one becomes at last truly settled, a coordinated, integrated personality.

This is the life beyond earnestness, beyond anxiety, beyond strain. Its strength sets in when we let go. This is a way fraught with danger, for it is easy to *deduce* human passivity from divine initiative. But the root *experience* of divine Presence contains within it not only a sense of being energized *from* a heavenly Beyond; it contains also a sense of being energized *toward* an earthly world. For the Eternal Life and Love are not pocketed in us; they are flooded *through* us into the world. There is an element of transmissiveness in the experience of being energized by the Divine Life... We are significant terminals of Love and Power, ends of Love; we are also transmitting channels, means and ends of creative Love. Through us the hungry world must be fed. We dare not oppose the divine urgency. Great things may be done for men, for we do not do them; they are done through us. We do not carry the load, in anxious balance. The living waters sweep through us to make green the fields of men. We are at peace. If we succeed, it is God who had succeeded, if we encounter defeat, then it is part of that strange resistance within History which God permits in a going world. Gladly we become anonymous, like the writer of the *Thelogia Germanica*, for to God belongs all the praise....

...The experience of the invading persuasion of Love points to an *objectivity*, a real dynamic power and Life working within us and through us, which is utterly alien to the subjectivity with which inner-light-teaching is so often charged. Indeed, it is "a beyond that is within," as Rufus Jones is fond to say...

...The beyond which is within opens up as yet another beyond, the world of earthly need and pain and joy and beauty. For the Inner Light illumines not only God but the world. Its discovery within ourselves does not insulate us, together with the Eternal, in solitary ecstasy, away from the poverties of earth; it opens our eyes to the old world and shows it to us in a new way.

Formerly the world spread itself out before us, focused about ourselves. We were the center. All our enjoyment, of things and men, was *for* us, to exploit, to rearrange, to clamber over, to conquer. The effective limits of our world were the limits of its utility or importance for us. The world-managing attitude has reigned with peculiar force in modern times, since Francis Bacon. And in this attitude, taken in solitary predominance, lie all the seeds of war, a *bellum omnium contra omnes*, as Thomas Hobbes called it. And in this world-managing epoch we all, as men and as nations, carry over into our working hours the phantasy-life of the daydreams, with its center in the conquering hero or the suffering hero. In this respect, modern man tends to be far indeed from that spirit which is near to the center of religion, the final joyful submission of all one's being to the Holy, the feeling of absolute dependence of Schleiermacher.

But in the Eternal Presence, the world spreads itself out, not as our little world, but as the world of God. And we sigh, at last we awake. And now we must say — it sounds blasphemous, but mystics are repeatedly charged with blasphemy — now we must say it is given to us to see the world's suffering, *throughout*, and bear it, Godlike, upon our shoulders, and suffer with all things and all men, and rejoice with all things and all men, and we see the hills clap their hands for joy, and we clap our hands with them. A friend has told me how it was given to her to see the entirety of the evil of the world, on its backside, so to say, and to look *through* it, into the face of God. That I have not seen. But suffering and the joy and the serenity at the heart of the world — these are unspeakably great. Were one not assisted, one could not bear it. It is an awful thing to fall into the hands of the living God. It was truly said by George Fox, "I was come up through the flaming sword into the paradise of God." But there is a point of vision from which one can look through sorrow and pain and still see the face of the Eternal Lover. This is a hard saying, but worthy of all acceptation.

It is frequently said that to bear this world, we must become toughened, callous, hard. The sadness of the city-evils, the blighted lives we see, the injustices, the pain and tears! Without a protective covering of indifference, it seems rational to say we cannot endure the world. But the Eternal Presence, shining upon time, gives us, not a tough protection, but an exquisitely *tendered* spirit. Overburdened men and women, blighted lives, slaveries in all their modern forms, nations and institutions in insane self-destruction, and little children hoping for warmth and love and opportunity [are all laid upon us]. To our easier sympathy with physical pain there is added suffering because of the soul-blindedness which we see everywhere. To see hatred poison a life is suffering indeed. The self-seeking, so-called "successful man," who has missed the holy way, who began to be a *Mann* and ended by being a *Kaufmann*, is as saddening as the drunkard or the criminal. In the figure of John Bunyan one says: Why do men rake together the sticks and straws of the world, when their heads are offered the crown of life! Before, our chief suffering, the suffering about which we are disturbed, was *our own* suffering. The world's arrows were thought to be aimed at us. But with the great unselfing, the center of concern for suffering is shifted *outside* ourselves and distributed with breadth unbounded among all, friends and so-called enemies. For a few agonized moments we may seem to be given to stand *within* the heart of the World-Father and feel the infinite sufferings of love toward all the Father's children. And pain inflicted on them becomes pain inflicted on ourselves. Were the experience not also an experience suffused with radiant peace and power and victory, as well as tragedy, it would be unbearable.

Have you experienced this tendering, this concern even for the sparrow's fall? For this is not a peculiar experience of Jesus. Neither is it an *inference* which we draw regarding the extent of the watchful love of God. It is the record of His life in God and it comes likewise to others in heartbreaking acuteness. Let me give John Woolman's account of an experience. "In a time of sickness a little more than two and a half years ago, I was brought so near the gates of death that I forgot my name. Being then desirous to know who I was, I saw a mass of matter, of a dull gloomy color between the south and the east, and was informed that this mass of human beings was in as great misery as they could be and yet live, and I was *mixed with them*, and that henceforth I might not consider myself as a distinct or separate being. In that state I remained for several hours. I heard a soft, melodious voice, more pure and harmonious than anything I had ever heard with ears before; I believe it was an angel that spoke to the other angels; the words were: 'John Woolman is dead.' " Intolerable sufferings of all mankind, and John Woolman "was mixed with them" until he cried: "I am crucified with Christ. Nevertheless I live, yet not I, but Christ liveth in me. And the life I now live in the flesh I live by faith of the Son of God, who loved me and gave himself for me. Then the mystery was opened and I perceived ... that the language 'John Woolman is dead' meant no more than the death of my own will."

To you I speak with much hesitation about

suffering. For I am only in middle years, and for me life has not been hard. But there is an introduction to suffering which comes with the birthpains of Love. And in such suffering one finds for the first time how deep and profound is the nature and meaning of life. And in such suffering one sees, as if one's eye were newly opened upon a blinding light, the very Life of the Eternal God Himself. And there too is suffering, but there, above all, is peace and victory.

Another aspect of the same awakening of the soultenderness is the new love of the world. Before, we had loved the world because it enriched our lives — we were the receiving centers. But now all is new, even the nature of love itself. Our families, our dear ones, they are reloved. For family love is now understood in the light of an Eternal Love that endures to the end for its beloved ones. And just as the infinite Love of God enfolds us, so we know that infinite Love enfolds all things in our love. Yet it is not our love but the love of God, loving its way, through us, to this world. Would that we could encounter all needs, bear all burdens, dry all tears, fulfill all... dreams. But the three-score years and ten close in upon us and the geographical and historical necessities put bounds upon us. Yet, in *intention*, we love all, suffer with all and rejoice with all, and laugh with all. In the tendering sense of the Eternal Presence we come to the burden-bearing, Calvary re-enacting life which is the heart of Christian living....

...Concerning the living Christ, I find it

difficult to make a special paragraph. For it is concerning Him that we have spoken throughout the entire discussion. ...He does not stand as one member of a series, but underlies all things; through Him all things were made; in Him was life, and the life was the Light of Men. (John 1:3-4.)

But in the dawning experience of the living Christ, the life, the teaching, and particularly the Cross and the triumph of Jesus of Nazareth became indescribably vivid and significant. For in Him the Divine Invasion... has taken place as never before, nor since, complete. And the world of human sin and human presumption stands out sharp, exposed, naked, in that blinding light of a revelation which exhibits the righteousness as well as the love of God. Through the inner revelation of the living Christ there has begun to dawn in us something of the communion between Love and Suffering and Burden-bearing.... In Him one sees these things grasped and embodied and lived out in time so amazingly that we stand in reverence and awe. And although we understand Him in part, through the Living Christ, yet we do not understand all. For the communion of Love and Suffering... and victory on the Cross contains the secret which leads back into the very nature of God Himself. And if the holy impulsion of the Eternal Presence, the Living Christ, any small hint of this divine secret is embodied in our own lives, still it is not conscious, external imitation, but a grace-given outflowing from the same wellsprings of Divine Life and Love as flowed so in Jesus of Nazareth.

Another fruit of the Eternal Presence is the enormous delight one finds in worship. And the quickening occurs both in private and in public worship. In private one walks and talks and sings with God, like a lover and a beloved. And along with such intimacy goes also an exalted wonder at the loftiness of God. One cries within oneself as is said in Isaiah: "I saw also the Lord, ... high and lifted up.... Holy, holy, holy, is the Lord of hosts: the whole earth is full of his glory" (6:1,3). Thanksgiving, prayer, praise, adoration, are breathed into us, and we breathe them back toward their source and goal.

But worship and praise in fellowship with others become enormously desired. The place of worship with one's fellows becomes Beth-el, the house of God. The day and the hour are longed for, with deep intensity. This fellowship in worship is not just an earthly reciprocal fellowship, but a fellowship wherein we pass beyond our separate selves into unity with that one Self, whom to know is life indeed. Bathed in such fellowship as includes the Beloved One and ourselves within one whole, our separate words lose their separateness, our gestures toward heaven, all pageantry of ritual are left behind, in living silence we lift our souls aloft, as one soul, in a common adoring silence, "lost in wonder, love and praise."

The peak or center of fellowship is experienced in common worship. There is a series, or progression from words, through gentle breathing, into silence. On the periphery we discuss, we argue, we talk, we analyze our problems. And this is proper and necessary. But torrents of words pour at the *periphery* of religious fellowship. One sign of the dilution of present-day Protestantism in America is the frequently encountered supposition that a religious gathering has been worthwhile if a good discussion has been set going. But beneath our exchange of words lies a Life, whose gentle persuasions need listening ears and sensitized souls to feel His unifying graciousness. As we near the center, words become weak and halting, obstructions rather than aids, and we sink into what an early Friend called the "gentle breathings" toward the Lord. Or, are they gentle breathings into us from beyond? The boundaries of selfhood seem weakened, and one can say *Es betet.* But at last comes even the end to articulate words. Silence of the outward is complete. Yet all the outward is in the Presence. Often a problem, personal or of the group, is carried into the [silence] and, as it were, held within the Presence. Without agonized reflection upon it at every moment we find afterward that the direction of its solution is clear in our minds. The Eternal Presence has particularized its wisdom and energy within the minds of the worshipers, sometimes as an individual judgment, sometimes as a group decision....

...In worship we have our neighbors to right and left, before and behind, yet the Eternal

44

Presence is over all and beneath all. Worship does not consist in achieving a mental state of concentrated isolation from one's fellows. But in the depth of common worship it is as if we found our separate lives were all one life, within whom we live and move and have our being. Communication seems to take place sometimes without words having been spoken. In the silence we received an unexpected commission to bear in loving intentness *and* spiritual need of another person sitting nearby. And that person goes away, uplifted and refreshed. Sometimes in that beautiful experience of living worship which the Friends have called "the gathered meeting," it is as if we joined hands and hearts, and lifted them together toward the unspeakable glory. Or it is as if that light and warmth dissolved us together into one. Tears are not to be scorned, then, for we stand together in the Holy of Holies. In hushed awe we wait, as the sacrament of the fellowship is enacted in our midst, and we feed on the body of the Lamb that was slain from the foundation of the world. In this true mass, the Host has been elevated over all, by a divine Ministrant. And we go forth, with hushed voices, and with power and peace and joy....

...A few weeks ago a man and his wife told me, with light in their eyes, how, three years ago, in the midst of their eighteen-year-old daughter's death had come to them the peace and Presence of the Great Companion, and had rebuilt them into lives of joyful service among young people of their daughter's generation...From such people time's arrows fall back, like the spear of Klingsor hurled at the heart of Parsifal.

"For I am persuaded, that neither death, nor life, nor angels, nor principalities, nor powers, nor things present, nor things to come, nor height, nor depth, nor any other creature, shall be able to separate us from the love of God, which is in Christ Jesus our Lord" (Rom. 8:38-39).

IV

Religion for this Distraught World

Only those whose spirits are pure gold can stand the atmosphere of today's distraught world. Religion itself is being tried and tested as by the refiner's fire. Minds are trained but ineffective because they are so open people cannot make decisions. Sometimes it is a good thing to close one's state of mind when certain principles have been accepted for a perpetual open-mindedness cannot be maintained with any goal-accomplishment. There is a need for positive drive and conviction. We are ready for new truth, but the old that is true must be kept, too. There is something deeper than doing. We must learn how to wait in quiet and not be always physically active. As a Western people we have a fear of a turned-in religion. We are constantly trying to be objective in our religious and intellectual life.

Religion must be able to enlist the whole of men — their spirit, their whole personality. Religion must bring unification within the individual and give direction to groups. It is that to which a life can be committed with all one's being. Jesus' concept of welding people in a spiritual sense was expressed in the phrase "the

Kingdom of God." The roots of this idea are eternal. Taken in its true and entire sense, such an idea seems too exacting and hard. Many of us prefer a simpler program. Jesus' conception of this phrase, however, would unify lives and bring new conceptions to mankind. Until the Christian Church returns to the conception that only those lives are pure gold which are wholly given to God, there will not be effective service to man or worthy fellowship with the Father.

Secular action is on the increase and religion as an influence is on the wane. Quakers appeared in history at just such a time as this, when the experience of deep religion had grown thin. Preachers lacked personal relationship with God. The Society of Friends arose to bring back vital apostolic power. The purpose was not to form another sect and to justify it by a peculiar tenet. Friends came to dig down to the wellsprings of spiritual immediacy, holding that religion means that which you know, feel, experience within yourself. Our task isn't to nurse the dying embers of a dying sect, but to be missionaries to Christendom; to live in a real Christian fellowship, not within a definite organization.

Religion means living and walking with God; experiencing the power and triumph of knowing Him — in short, living in the sense of the imminence of God. Fountains of Divine apostolic strength can burst forth for us all and permit us to live in fellowship with God. The time has come when men must recognize the total-itarian claims of the gospel, when they must live lives of as complete dedication as did monks in the Middle Ages, renouncing patterns of ambition.

St. Francis came nearer than has any other man to reliving the life of Jesus. He was a personality that radiated gentleness, power, and joy. His nature awoke such reverberations of loyalty that his followers formed orders of men and women which were to emulate his life. Some of these were patterned upon withdrawal from the world, but most of his followers he sent back to their native villages and communities to live with their families lives of service and frugality. These were Franciscans of the Heart — folk whose cells were within themselves and who lived God-given lives in the midst of everyday problems while earning their living and that of their families. We need such a "third order" today, and there is such an order among us made up of people who have a quiet spot of peace in their own beings. For all such, life has become evaluated for they have at last looked upon the face of the Almighty. For them the world is neither to be hated nor shunned. They neither seek nor abhor fame. A dedicated life can be lived in the midst of poverty or plenty. Environment doesn't really matter.

A man should be so clothed in God that no one can reach Him without touching His coat. It is an area of our will, and not merely an intellectual vivisection of problems, that we are talking about here. We need to know the depth of love and suffering, to keep the cross shining in our interior cell until we know its meaning. We will then have a totalitarian commitment to God. The most fundamental thing anyone can do is to bring a man into the presence of God, and leave him there.

V

Where Are the Springs of Hope?

A year and a half ago I rode in a limousine in Germany from the home of a former Jewish millionaire, to the railroad station of a nearby city. Three Jews were with me, two of them were young rabbis, the third a man of wealth and influence. Today one of those young rabbis is dead, dead solely because of a broken heart, dead because the suffering of his people broke his health. The second has been stripped of his wealth and has lain in a concentration camp. The third, a young rabbi, a mystic who would be profoundly at home in a Quaker meeting, has been sucked into the maelstrom of Poland. If he is still alive, which is problematical, he is in poverty in a ghetto, or in enforced slavery within the German Reich. I dare not give more details about him lest he be alive and lest he be identified, even though these words are spoken here in Philadelphia, and disappear from the scene as I understand all persons mentioned in Nora Waln's book *Reaching for the Stars* have been identified and have utterly vanished.

In such a world as ours today, no light glib word of hope dare be spoken. Some of us hesitate to write to our friends in Europe, lest our words ring hollow in the ears of those who have heard deeper notes of suffering than you or I have ever known. And the same is even truer of our letters to our friends in China and Japan in these days. Only the most searching integrity, only the willingness to go to the absolute bottom of life's vase, gives us the right to talk of hope. Only if we look long and deeply into the abyss of despair do we dare to speak of hope. Only as we know a deeper ground of uncertainty, that can stand *every* privation and atrocity of which we have read, can stand them as *committed upon ourselves and upon our families*, and can still rise radiant and triumphant, dare we speak a word of hope. We dare not tell men to hope in God or in Christ unless we know what it means to have absolutely no other hope but in Him. But as we know something of such a profound and amazing assurance, clear at the depths of our beings, then we dare to proclaim it boldly in the midst of a world aflame. But the words are no good if the life experience is not behind them.

A friend of mine tells me how, when he was penniless and on the verge of starvation in the city of Milan, in Italy, an American tourist glibly told him to trust in God, and he tells how he cursed her with all the vehemence of his soul.

Quick relief from the ghastly tragedy of war may be promised by a truce. But such a truce, with the seeds of war still germinating, is only an interlude between wars. Political schemes of Union Now are empty *if* the will to the good of all is not genuinely beneath them. Greater intelligence in the direction of human affairs is not sufficient ground of hope, if the motivations of the heart are not transformed. Collective security and massed armaments controlled by a central power will be only the dragon's teeth sown in the soil of national hatreds and jealousies. No, our *final* hope is not here. Our task is deeper yet. Our task is to produce men and women of utterly new motivation, and social patterns, such as the concept of nationhood on a wholly new basis.

We are men of double personalities. We have slumbering demons within us. We all have also a dimly-formed Christ within us. We've been too ready to say that the demonic man within us is the natural and the real man, and that the Christ-man within us is the unnatural and the unreal self. But the case is that our surface potentialities are for selfishness and greed, for tooth and claw. But deep within, in the whispers of the heart, is the surging call of the Eternal Christ, hidden within us all. By an inner isthmus we are connected with the mainland of the Eternal Love. Surface living has brought on the world's tragedy. Deeper living leads us to the Eternal Christ, hidden in us all. Absolute loyalty to this inner Christ is the only hope of a new humanity. In the clamor and din of the day, the press of Eternity's warm love still whispers in each of us, as our deepest selves, as our truest selves. Attend to the Eternal that He may recreate you and sow you deep into the furrows of the world's suffering.

At the time of the Day of Broken Glass in

Germany, the Arbeitsaus schuss or executive committee of the German Yearly Meeting was meeting in Bad Pyrmont. At that meeting was read the latter part of the 126th Psalm, which contains these words: "They that go forth in tears, *bearing their seed with them,* shall return in joy."

The important thing here is the phrase, "bearing their seed with them." Only those who go forth in tears, and who bear with them into their suffering some awakened seed, shall return in hope.

There is nothing automatic about suffering, so that suffering infallibly produces great souls. We have passed out of the prewar days when we believed in the escalator theory of progress. Those were the boom days of economic and churchly prosperity, when we thought that every day in every way we were growing better and better and we thought that the Kingdom of God on earth was just around the corner, if we, in *laisse faire* style, cooperated and didn't halt the process. Then it seemed easy to speak words of hope and to prod the last laggards into feverish activity to run the last mile of the race to the millennium. But now in the light of world war we are forced to abandon that easy view and go infinitely deeper. Now that suffering is upon the world we cannot appeal to the escalator theory of suffering and expect that suffering will inevitably shake great souls into life. No, there is nothing about suffering such that it automatically purges the dross from human nature and brings heroic souls upon the scene. Suffering can blast and blight an earnest but unprepared soul, and damn it utterly to despair.

No, only those who go into the travail of today, *bearing a seed within them*, a seed of awareness of the heavenly dimensions of humanity, can return in joy. Where this seed of divine awareness is quickened and grows, there Calvary is enacted again in joy. And Calvary is still the hope of the world. Each one of us has the seed of Christ within him. In each one of us the amazing and dangerous seed of Christ is present. It is only a seed. It is very small, like the grain of mustard seed. The Christ that is formed in us is small indeed, but He is great with eternity. But if we dare to take this awakened seed of Christ into the midst of the world's suffering, it will grow. That's why the Quaker work camps are important. Take a young man or young woman in whom Christ is only dimly formed, but one in whom the seed of Christ is alive. Put him into a distressed area, into a refugee camp, into a poverty region. Let him go into the world's suffering, bearing this seed with him, and in suffering it will *grow*, and Christ will be more and more fully formed in him. As the grain of mustard seed grew so large that the birds found shelter in it, so the man who bears an awakened seed into the world's suffering will grow until he becomes a refuge for many.

This is one of the springs of hope — the certainty that the seed of Christ is in us all (Quakers have also called it the inner light) and the confidence that many of those who call themselves Christian will enter suffering, bearing this seed with them, *daring* to let it germinate, *daring* to let it take them through personal risk and financial loss and economic insecurity, up the steep slopes of some obscure Calvary. Ponder this carefully: our right to life, liberty, and the pursuit of happiness is not absolute. We dare not claim them as our absolute right. For the seed of Christ that we bear into the world's suffering will teach us to *renounce* these as our own, and strip us, in utter poverty of soul and perhaps of body, until our only hope is in the eternal goodness of God.

In you is this seed. Do you not feel its quickening Life? Then, small though this seed be in you, sow your life into the furrows of the world's suffering, and you will return in joy, and the world will arise in hope. For Christ is born again, and is dying again on Calvary and rising victorious from the tomb.

The second spring of hope is this: We simple, humble men can bear the seed of hope. No religious dictator will save the world; no giant figure of heroic size will stalk across the stage of history today, as a new Messiah. But in simple, humble, imperfect men like you and me wells up the spring of hope. We have this treasure of the seed in the earthen vessels — very earthen vessels. You and I know how imperfect we are. And yet those little demonstrations of love and goodwill, such as the feeding of children in Spain, the direction of transit stations for refugees in Holland and Cuba, the reconstruction of lives in the coal fields, are being carried on by just such earthen vessels. These tasks shine like tiny candles in the darkness — deeds done in the midst of suffering, through which shines the light of the Living Christ, deeds that stir hope that humanity as a whole will be aroused to yield to the press and surge of the Eternal Love within them. For the Eternal Love is beating in upon us, upon you and upon me, quickening the seed within us into life. Our very weakness, as humans, is the fit soil for divine awakening. If you are proud and self-confident and sure you are no earthen vessel, then the greatness of the divine fructifying power will never be awakened in you. Yield yourselves to the growth of the seed within you, in these our days of suffering. Sow yourselves into the furrows of the world's pain, and hope will grow and rise high. Be not overcome by the imposing forces of evil and of might. Be of good cheer, says Jesus, *I have overcome the world.* But there is no hope if Calvary is only an external Calvary. Within you must the living Christ be formed, until you are led within yourselves to die wholly that you may wholly live. Then will Christ again walk the ways of the world's sorrows. In Him alone, and in you so far as Christ is formed in you, is the hope of the world. There is no cheaper hope than Calvary, no panacea other than awakened love that leads us into the world's suffering into victory.

PART TWO

The Publishers
of Truth

The articles here are directed to the nature and problems of the Society of Friends. But, as in all his writing, Thomas Kelly seems to transcend the immediate subject of his discussion, and non-Friends will find that his message to his own denomination applies to them as well.

"The Quaker Discovery" appeared in The Friend, *December, 1939. "Quakers and Symbolism" was written in early 1938 for presentation at the Green Street Meeting in Philadelphia. "The Gathered Meeting" was printed in pamphlet form and in* The Friend, *December, 1940. The term "Publishers of Truth" applies to the early Quaker leaders in seventeenth-century England and forms the title of this part and the final article which is an extract of an address to a Philadelphia Yearly Meeting group and published in the* Friends Intelligencer, *March, 1940.*

I

The Quaker Discovery

A great light and spiritual power blazed out in England, beginning about 1650, which shook thousands of their complacent formalism, which kindled men and women with radiant fires of divine glory and holy joy. It sent them out into the market places and the churches , ablaze with the message of the greatness and the nearness of God, His ready guidance and His enfolding love. The blazing light illuminated the darkness, the shams, the silly externalities of conventional religion. It threw into sharp relief the social injustices, the underpaying of servants, the thoughtless luxuries, the sword as an instrument of social or "Christian" justice.

You and I exist today as paled-out remnants of the movement which sprang out of that discovery and that light. Those fires of 1650 and 1660 flicker low. We are for the most part respectable, complacent, comfortable, with a respectable past, proud of our birthright membership in the Society of Friends which guarantees us entrance, if not into heaven, at least into very earthly society. The blazing, burning fires of three centuries ago are too generally sunk in us to a genial, mellow glow of historical sweetness and innocence and gentle beauty. And all too many of us, Quakers, near-Quakers, non-Quakers, have become as mildly and conventionally religious as were the tepid church members of three centuries ago against whose flaccid mediocrity Fox flung himself with all the passion and the energy which a new discovery unleashes in an awakened soul.

But the blazing discovery which Quakers made, long ago, is rediscovered again and again by individuals, and sometimes by groups. The embers flare up, the light becomes glorious. There is no reason why it cannot break out again, today, with blazing power. The world needs it desperately. It is in the hope that *you and I*, today, may rediscover this flaming center of religion that those words are written — not in an historical interest in a charming past. All that I would say to you about the past is directed to you in the present. Ask yourself: Am *I* down in the flaming center of God? Have *I* come into the deeps, where the soul meets with God and knows His Love and power? Have *I* discovered God as a living Immediacy, a sweet Presence and a stirring, life-renovating Power within me? Do I walk by His guidance, feeding every day, like knights of the Grail, on the body and blood of Christ, knowing every day and every act to be a sacrament?

George Fox was like most of us in his youth. He was a good person. He was a conscientious person. In his teens he was so religious, according to ordinary standard, that people thought he ought to study for the ministry (perhaps "at Oxford or Cambridge"). He says in his *Journal*: "As I grew up, my relations thought to make me a priest, but others persuaded to the contrary, whereupon I was put to a man, a shoemaker by trade and who dealt in wool, and used grazing and sold cattle."

But something told him there was something deeper to be found than he knew and than many respectable Christians knew who took their religious profession so lightly. He tells how, at the age of nineteen, he was shocked and revolted by the crass beer drinking of some respectable Christians who tried to entangle him in an ale-drinking bout. I believe *many* young people of tender vision and fresh sense of lofty, holy claims of God upon their lives are shocked by some of us who have good reputations but who have adjusted ourselves to conventional ways, and lowered our standards of dedication to God, and are stained with the mud of mediocrity.

That night he could not sleep but "walked up and down, and sometimes prayed and cried to the Lord who said unto me, 'Thou seest how young people go together into vanity and old people go into the earth.' " I take the phrase, "old people go into the earth," not to mean "go into the grave," but to mean, "go into earthiness." It is tragic to see middle-aged people "go into the earth." It grieved Fox's soul. Over the horizons of his consciousness he saw something, dim but glorious, that condemned his present state and the lethargy of his fellows, that led him on to deep questing for fuller life with God.

The quest so possessed him, body and soul, that he gave himself up wholly to it. "Then at the command of God, on the ninth day of the seventh month, I left my relations, and broke off all familiarity or fellowship with old or young. I passed to Lutterworth, where I stayed some time; then to Northampton, where also I made some stay; then to Newport Pagnell, whence, after I had stayed a while, I went to Barnett, in the fourth month called June 1644. As I thus traveled through the counties, professors took notice, and sought to be acquainted with me; but I was afraid of them, for I was sensible they did not possess what they professed."

This earnestness and thoroughness of search for that light, that religious depth which he glimpsed over the horizon, is something that *needs* to be engaged in. Almost all great souls have only achieved their illumination after a storm and stress period of the spirit. Yet we, many of us, halt before we enter such a deeper quest, such as Fox's. Our families tells us, "Take it mildly. Don't get unbalanced." And who knows how many of us have been halted and choked by older people's counsel to sobriety? Heaven knows Quakerism in later years has become stuffy with sobriety! Or our own sense of conventionality, or the molds of society, or the demand for earthly security, for earning a living and being normally equipped with an automobile and a nice home keep us from following out, with all the sincerity of our souls, this search for the deepest depths of religion.

Fox's own friends and relations tried to get him steady and sober, so that he might be a good shoemaker and forget his passionate search. "My relations would have had me marry, but I told them I was but a lad and I must get wisdom. Others would have had me in the Auxiliary Band among the soldiery but I refused, and I was grieved that they proffered such things to me, being a tender youth." Fox refused to be "toughened up" for the world's dullness by going into the army. He was tender, and he seemed to know, better than his elders, that the route to release lay in increase of that tenderness of spirit, not in its loss. And he was right. For sensitiveness to God's revealing Life requires a tendered soul.

In these years of deep searching Fox tried every spiritual guide he could get. Whenever he heard of a man, a minister or a layman, who had a reputation for deep, religious insight, he went to see him, to find if he could give him help. Even London yielded him no great soul to guide him. "I was under great misery and trouble there; for I looked upon the professors of the city of London, and I saw all was dark and under the chain of darkness." He went to the parish priest of his birthplace, but soon found that he, Fox, was giving the priest material for his sermons, rather than being instructed by the priest. "He would applaud and speak highly of me to others; and what I said in discourse to him on the weekends he would preach of on the First days; for which I did not like him." Another priest to whom he went for help into the inner sanctuary of religion advised him to smoke tobacco and sing psalms. But, he says: "Tobacco was a thing I did not love, and psalms I was not in a state to sing." One man, he comments, proved to be a hollow cask, another grew angry when he stepped on the edge of a flower bed, another told him he needed medicine and a blood-letting.

What was it that disturbed him during this period? It was not a deep sense of personal sin. He is singularly free from any feeling of sin. It was not the hounding of an evil conscience, the deep-voiced bayings of remorse. It was, I believe, two things. It was the deep God-hunger within him, on behalf of himself and on behalf of others. And it was the keen sorrow he felt at the sight of others, and himself, living in blindness and suffering, because they were missing the Way, dully unaware that there was a Way to seek. He saw professing Christians to be blinded, sinful, mediocre, walking habits, in a day when the fire had gone out of the church of Christ, and they were living, dead shadows, among the shadows of a past tradition, a past instruction, a past visitation of Pentecostal power and holiness.

Thus he was driven from all outer aids, and was forced back *within* himself for *inner* insights and guidance. The very first constructive insight, the first inward ray of light which he reports, has to do with the *whole of Christendom*, the entire Christian Church. "About the beginning of 1646, as I was going to Coventry, and entering towards the gates, a consideration arose in me, how it was said that all Christians are believers, both Protestants and Papists; and the Lord opened to me that, if all were believers, then they were all born of God, and passed from death to life, and that none were true believers but such; and though others said they were believers, yet were they not."

This was not a narrowing of the gate of Truth. Fox had no thought of or interest in founding a little sect which should play upon a single string and call its music the whole of truth. *All* are in the life of God, whether Protestant or Catholic, who have been "born of God," who have been brought into God's immediate fellowship, who have become sons of God (for whom, as Paul says, the whole creation groaneth and travaileth in pain, until such be born). And none who have never been brought into God's immediacy are even Christians at all, no matter if they are members of a church and have the best gilt-edged credentials of an outward sort. Religion is in nothing outward; no church can save us. Religion is *inward*, it arises in immediacy of relation with God. It involves new blood in our veins. It involves the lifeblood of each of us, so that we can say, "My Father. I am in His family. I have fellowship in His love."

Another dawning insight which broke in upon him was that there is no substitute for *immediacy of revelation*. Each individual soul must be and can have direct illumination inside himself, from the living, revealing Spirit of God, now, today, for He is active in the world. The form of this dawning insight in Fox had to do with what fitted a man to be a minister. He says, "At another time, as I was walking in a field on a First Day morning, the Lord opened to me that being bred at Oxford or Cambridge was not enough to fit and qualify men to be ministers of Christ." That is to say, in modern terms: You can go to theological seminary, and study *about* religion. You can learn the history of the Christian Church. You can know all about the Synoptic problems of the Gospels and have your own theories about Q and the J, E, D and P document of the Hexateuch, you can know all the literature about the authorship of the Johannine epistles, whether the author was John the beloved disciple or another of the same name. You can know all about the history of Quakerism, you can know the disputes behind the Nicene Creed and the Constantinopolitan Creed. You can know the Westminster Confession and the Augsburg Confession and the Thirty-nine Articles of the Church of England. You can know homiletics and rules of good sermon structure. You can know church symbolism and the meaning of the feasts and fasts of the church. You can know all this, and much more. But unless you *know God*, immediately, every day communing with Him, rejoicing in Him, exalting in Him, opening your life in Joyful obedience toward Him and feeling Him speaking to you and guiding you into ever fuller loving obedience to Him, you aren't fit to be a minister. There is so much that is wonderful in books. But he who relies for his sermons upon bookstuff *about* religion, and is not at the same time enjoying immediately and experiencing vitally fresh illumination from God, is not a real minister, even if he has a degree in theology from Oxford or Cambridge. Secondhand sermons aren't *real* sermons. Only firsthand preaching counts. He is a minister who is given a message within himself, as a fresh insight from God, transmitted *through Him* to others.

Another insight which came to him had to do with churches and temples. The church building is not a church, the brick and mortar structure is not a church. God doesn't live in a house with a peaked roof. God lives inside people. And if God isn't inside you, you needn't expect to find him in a house with a peaked roof that is outside you. God is within. And where He dwells, there is a holy place. Fox was finding he had an altar inside his own soul. Inside him was a hushed and holy Presence, too sacred to be destroyed, too wonderful not to be visited continually. The holy Presence was Inward. Fox found Him there, and all life was new. It is a wonderful discovery , to find that you are a temple, that you have a church *inside* you, where God is. There is something awful, that is, awe-inspiring, down at the depths of our own soul. In hushed silence attend to it. It is a whisper of God Himself, particularizing Himself for you and in you, and speaking to the world through you. God isn't dead. "The Lord is in his holy temple; let all the earth keep silence before him."

All of these insights are such as wean us away from confusing religious information with external things, with external church membership, with external church doctrines, external church habitations. In place of these, Fox went inward, and there found resplendent glory of God's immediacy and love and power and guidance and sufficiency. And this is a true insight, which finds the inner sanctuary of the soul to be the Home of God. As long as outwards are counted as essential, we are no better than those reported by the Samaritan woman to Jesus: "Shall we worship in this mountain or in Jerusalem?" Shall we perform this ceremony or that? Shall we assent to this statement or a different one? Christianity needs to get behind its still lingering confusion about the essential character of *any* external, even as beautiful as that of dramatizing the Lord's supper with His disciples, and put first of all the sacrament of the heart, where God and man break bread together in the secret sanctuary of the soul.

Fox might seem to have retained reliance upon one outward guide, the Scriptures. He lived with his Bible. He studied it day and night. But the Scriptures, too, were no outward guide to him. He came to see that one needed to get back into that Spirit and that Life which the writers of the Scriptures knew and in which they lived. And when one gets back into that Life and Spirit in which the Scriptures were given forth, one understands them, as it were, from within. Quakers make a special approach to the Bible. Not merely by exegesis, not merely by grammar and Greek lexicon do we squeeze out the meaning of the texts, not merely understanding the historical setting of a book like Amos or Hosea or Isaiah do we find its meaning. We can go back into that Life within whom Amos and Isaiah lived, that Life in God's presence and vivid guidance, then we understand the writings from within. For we and Isaiah and Hosea feed on the same Life, are rooted in the same holy flame which is burning in our hearts. And we speak, each for his day, out of the same center, in God. "But I brought them Scriptures and told them there was an anointing within man to teach him, and that the Lord would teach His people Himself."

This last phrase might almost sum up the central discovery of George Fox. "The Lord has come to teach His people Himself." Like a refrain it runs through early Quaker literature: "The Lord has come to lead His people Himself." No longer do we rely upon creeds or priests to be our external guides. "The Lord has come to lead His people Himself." No longer are we shut up to exegeting passages from an ancient text. "The Lord has come to teach His people himself." No longer do we say that revelation is closed, that Heaven has finished her instruction to men, that God is absent and Christ is withdrawn. "The Lord has come to teach His people Himself."

This was a burning experience to Fox. He had a teacher within him. He found God alive, at work, a living, pulsing, soul-enlarging, holy Life within him, guiding and instructing, not in general terms, but in specific terms, for him, George Fox. This is so different from the generalized instruction of universal truths. Here we have divine guidance particularized for you, for me. The Quaker discovery includes the fact of immediate guidance possible to be experienced within each of us. But until each of us can say, "The Lord has come to lead His people, *and He is leading me*," we are merely reading about an interesting historical event in the life of Fox.

Fox was pretty well through with his agony of search. God, immediate, amazing, radiant, was dawning in some of His matchless glory. But he still had his ups and downs, of sorrow and joy, depressions over deficiencies and elations over the light and glory of God. "I kept myself much as a stranger, seeking heavenly wisdom and getting knowledge from the Lord; and was brought off from outward things, to rely wholly on the Lord alone. Though my exercises and troubles were very great, yet were they not so continual but that I had some intermissions, and was sometimes brought into such heavenly joy, that I thought I had been in Abraham's bosom."

But there must have been some last lingering reserve within him which had not yet yielded to the divine Light. Somewhere he must still have kept some hope of help from outside himself, still hoping someone would give him the great advice, would speak the solving word which would lead him fully into the divine Center of life in the presence of God. But finally the last vestige of external hope was gone. Like so many great religious souls, he had to be brought to utter exhaustion before the complete filling by God could set in. Too many of us have never pursued after God till we are at this point of utter exhaustion. Too many of us have easily stilled the God-hunger in our hearts. Too many of us rely upon God to do a few things for us, while we feel able to take care of the rest. But Fox followed clear to the end of a complete disenchantment. He found nothing in the outer world, nothing in himself as a man, to bring him to his Home. And when he surrendered, God came in wholly and in flooding love and joy and peace. "When all my hopes in them and in all men were gone, so that I had nothing outward to help, nor could I tell what to do, then, O! then I heard a voice which said, 'There is one, even Christ Jesus, that can speak to thy condition.' And when I heard it my heart did leap for joy."

This was the final release, the entrance upon the full, amazing life for which he had yearned as a nineteen-year-old boy, for which he had sought for seven or eight years in increasing inwardness. At last it was not he that searched; it was God who was active in him. The center shifted from himself to God. He passed out of subjective yearning into energizing from beyond, yet a beyond that was within. "Thus when God doth work, who shall let it? And this I knew experimentally." He knew experimentally what it meant to find that God invaded the soul with a breath-taking rush, crowding all else out, leaving no room for any but Himself. "This I knew experimentally." This, I take it, was an experience of power, the irresistible power of God. It comes to us at last, at the end of the search. When He comes in, power comes in. And when He came in, fully, when the last reserve in him was gone, Fox knew a new power in living. He became a triumphant, victorious, conquering personality. Men cowered before his piercing eyes as before the penetrating eyes of God, that look through all shams. The heaven-guided life is a life of power, triumphant, amazing, victorious, power. Fox discovered it himself; he saw that power working outside him, in others. He relied upon it.

His experience of power was tempered by an overwhelming experience of the *love* of God. "At another time I saw the great love of God, and I was filled with admiration at the infiniteness of it.... One day I was walking solitarily abroad, and was coming home, I was taken up in the love of God, so that I could not but admire the greatness of His love."

And in the power and the vigor and the confidence of the Apostolic days, he and his followers set out to restore the Christian Church to its lost vigor and life. The early Quakers were founding no sect; they were reforming Christendom, that had slumped into externals and had lots its true sense of the immediate presence and the creative, triumphant power of the living God within us all. They had a message for all, for they had discovered that "the Lord Himself had come to lead His people."

And in that same way the Quaker discovery, not of a doctrine, not of a belief, but of a Life, a life filled with God, a life listening, obedient, triumphant, holy — in that same way the Quaker discovery was only a rediscovery of the life and power and fellowship and joy and radiance which moved the early Church. Its rediscovery today is desperately needed, for the fellowship of believers has grown dim, and only a few clear voices ring out in the twilight. You and I *can* be the instruments of the opening of God's life. But it is heroic work, not work for the milder Quaker. The fires of God burn bright . In their light we are judged or consumed, in their light the world is condemned. In their light we may discover what so many have really lost, namely, God Himself. And what is a greater discovery?

II

Quakers and Symbolism

Not shadow but substance, not symbols but the Reality they signify! Such is the true cry of the soul who comes to himself and longs for God, and for God alone. No stony substitutes for bread will appease. All veils must disappear, all mediations must be left behind. We must stand and walk and bask and nestle in the Unspeakable Presence itself. In unutterable sweetness we walk in heavenly places in Christ Jesus and see things which it is not lawful for men to utter.

Grounded in such experience of immediacy, Friends have discounted and discredited the *symbolic* in religion. Crucifixes and swinging censers, incense and the elevation of the Host in the Mass, prostration of the body as token of humility of heart before God, liturgical pageantry which dramatizes the aspiration and the response of God, conventionalized enactment of bodily washing as a symbol of an inner cleansing—these and many more formal symbols, such as creedal expression of the solidarity of a particular Christian community, have been rejected by Friends. They have been dismissed as shadows because the substance of the Bread of Life is at hand.

It is the vivid sense of the immediacy of men's access to God which makes symbols seem unnecessary. Symbols seem to have an implication of *remoteness*. They seem to be gestures of *aspiration*, wavings of the spirit across far-distant spaces toward a remoter Deity, confessions of hope, and desire, and postponed fulfillment. But one breath of *immediacy* makes symbols obstructive, misleading, encumbering. When we are in the presence of our Father, we no longer need His photograph. We enjoy the Father Himself. And in joy we sit in the Holy Presence in worship, and in joy we walk the streets with lighted footsteps, and in serene peace we sleep in His bosom at night.

But there is a second reason for Friends' distrust of symbols. Symbols are stationary, unchanging, frozen, while the Life of the Spirit which they symbolize is flowing, growing, changing, ever becoming richer. If we were successful, in any moment, in devising a symbolic expression absolutely adequate to represent the richness of our soul's experience of the Divine Life, then the next moment, and certainly the next day and the next year will find that symbol to be in some degree inadequate, antiquated, obsolete. For the Spirit's working, if we keep alive and sensitive to Him, is ever leading us into new vistas of truth, where the pastures become greener and the still waters greater beneath their limpid mirror.

The tension between the static symbol and the dynamic flow of religious experience, mild at first, becomes acute and disastrous. The pot-bound plant exhibits the tension between the dynamic pressure of life and the static confinement of unchanging form. In time either the life will wither and die or the pot will be shattered by the life that it thought to contain. A better metaphor is that of the skin of the moulting insect or snake. For the confining skin at one time fitted the animal nicely — was in fact in exact conformity to its latest stage of development. But life, insistent, sinuous, expanding, makes the waistcoat grow tighter, and kindly nature provides that the encompassing shell shall not grow so strong as to restrain forever the pressure toward revision of form.

The postulate, and the experience which underlies the tension between symbol and the Reality symbolized, is that of *growing* religious life. Were life to cease at the point of symbolic creation, *no tension would arise at all.* In him for whom the fires of faith have turned to embers there is no chill in religious symbols — for him they suggest muffled reverberations of sweet footsteps once present, but long since passed away in fading echoes.

The recognition of a *flowing* at the heart of our world is seen within the Greek Heraclitus, for whom no man goes down the same river twice; it is vivid for the Chinese who make the dragon with its sinuous curves and endless motion stand for the inner vision of *change* at the heart of all things; it is the central contention of Bergson that the essentially real is *time*, duration at its flow, which can never be caught and imprisoned within inflexible concepts. But the religious man has found something still deeper than merely that "time like an ever-rolling stream bears all her sons away." Movement *from beyond* is within, in immediacy of guidance. To the quickening of *that* movement the Friend would respond, and cleave to it forever in its creative work in the world. Not the movement of time, but the movement of the Eternal in the midst of time, is the ground of tension between symbol and that religious experience which lives and moves in the awareness of an unutterable, dynamic, moving, creative Presence. It is a Presence which engenders a peace surpassing all understanding, but which yet puts the fire and the hammer into one's soul. For him who knows at first hand the Eternal One steadfastly breaking into time at that point which is the depth of his own consciousness — for him any symbol whatever which he chooses, with which to clothe his expanding and unutterable experience, will be quickly transcended and outgrown.

But the fact remains that symbolism is an enormously bulky and persistent aspect of religion, in all parts of the world, when the echoes of the fading footsteps of the founders have died away from the corridors and the croaking of imitators has begun. The symbolic breaking of bread in a common meal was practiced in glowing devotion by the early church, in the directness and simplicity of a reverential church supper long before the practice became conventionalized as the Mass. It behooves us therefore: (a) to inquire what underlies the impulse to symbolize in order to see whether that impulse inheres in the very essence of religion, or is an accidental accompaniment; (b) to inquire whether Friends themselves reject *all* symbolism or only certain forms of symbolism while necessarily retaining others; and (c) to inquire about the *media* in which symbolism is embodied, and ask if Friends have not laid hold upon a medium of dynamic symbolism that is deep and rich and true, and relatively free from the dangers of rigid symbols.

But first let us be clear what we have in mind when we speak of *symbols*. The usual symbols Quakers talk against are the two sacraments, of baptism and the Lord's Supper. With it, of course, goes all the pageantry of liturgical drama and vestments. But in theological usage *written creeds* are also called symbols. But in addition, there is a still wider meaning to symbols, namely, our *language*. Our words are *conventional symbols* of meaning. By means of words we gesture *beyond* those words to the realities *meant* by those words. We can thus distinguish between the more limited symbolism of the ordinances, ritual and creeds, and wider symbolism inevitably involved in *the very use of words at all*.

And one characteristic of all symbols is that they gesture *beyond themselves*. They step aside, once our attention has been, by them, directed beyond themselves. Their value is *instrumental*, lying beyond themselves, rather than *intrinsic*, lying within themselves alone.

What underlies the impulse to symbolism? I should answer: the *impulse to communicate*, to share experience with another. The commonest and most widespread use of symbols, namely language, rests upon just this profound fact of man's nature — his impulse to share his values with others. Symbols are media of communication of the riches of the spirit. Where a great and wonderful enriching discovery is made, there is the impulse to communicate it or bestir it in others. This impulse to *share* our values is certainly near the heart of religious experience. Religious experience is tinged, deeply dyed, with *sociality*. As the desire to enjoy a sunrise with another makes us gesture toward the sky, so a discovery of the glory of God in the midst of mundane life draws us to others, and across the spaces which seem to separate our personal lives we gesture to the sunrise and the Dayspring from on high which has visited us. Surely in this sense Friends are as *communicative* as any other religious group, and know these joyous bonds of shared values. And conversely, where we have no impulse to *communicate*, to share our *good news* (i.e., Gospel), there it is doubtful whether there is any living good news to share.

Symbols, however, are not for their own sake, but the sake of that reality which is meant by them. When we point our friend to the rising sun we mean for him to glance at our finger and thence to the glory itself. The mediation is for the sake of immediacy. Once the sun is seen, the finger is no longer needed. Once we have passed, in group worship, beyond words and symbols, we sit down together in heavenly places in Christ Jesus. But many a man and woman, and boy and girl, has been pointed beyond his petty preoccupations to the Light of Lights, by the broken, halting words of some man who has seen the glory. In this sense of symbolism, as the use of words to point beyond words, Quakers practice symbolism, for we still believe profoundly in what Paul calls "the foolishness of preaching."

Every sermon or utterance is a gesture of the spirit toward an experience other than the mere experience of hearing the words. We must resort to the mediation of symbols, for *immediacy cannot be communicated*. But all such mediation of words is for the sake of stimulating others to pass beyond our words, and theirs, into that Immediacy wherein is fullness of life. Thus preaching in words springs out of immediacy, gives rise to mediation (by words) which point back to immediacy. It is of the essence of Quakerism *not to get far from home base*, to be chary of venturing very far away from the immediate upspringings of life. Yet it is also of the essence of Quakerism, as of all true religion, to seek to communicate its vision to others, and thereby to venture upon symbolism, especially the symbolism involved in *words*. Here is a paradoxical inner tension in religious experience. We must *advance* verbal, intellectual descriptions of our immediate experience, directed toward others, and toward our other inward selves. There is rightly an intellectual element in religion which we cannot avoid. But we are forever *renouncing* our words and passing credos as insufficient, and crowding back into that sweet Life which gave them forth. The Quaker makes a *restrained* use of symbolism, the barely necessary minimum, fearful of its dangers, while other religious groups make *luxuriant* use of symbolism, and seek to guard against its dangers.

And the danger in symbols which Quakers fear is that *life* will go out of the symbol, leaving it an empty shell, a static form, cruelly confining or killing out the living movement of the spirit.

Those religious groups which practice elaborate symbolism in worship are, for the most part, as keenly aware as are the Friends of the danger that life will go out of the symbol, and leave only the form, mistaken for the substance. It is not Quakers alone who know it is hypocritical to point others to the sunrise when you have ceased to see it yourself. But ritualistic groups believe that the symbol is increasingly invested with meaning, while Quakers believe that the symbol is increasingly *divested* of meaning as time goes by. The ritualists presume the symbol to be *ahead* of the present development of most members of a group, the product of the spiritual creativity of discerning leaders. Quakers reject the aristocratic implications of this view, look upon any presently developed symbol as merely of the present, ready quickly to lapse into the past as outgrown. The ritualist sees in his symbols a point of attachment for the increasing winnings of spiritual development, so that the crucifix and the liturgy and the prayer book *grow*, by accretions of association, with the growth of increasingly religious experience, and cease, in some measure at least, to be the static structures the Quakers fear. But the Quaker wants to have symbol and reality in religious experience keep pace with each other, not by *importing into* stationary symbols some growth of meaning, but by recreating his symbols to keep pace with the moving life of the Spirit.

But if Friends perforce must retain the use of the symbol structure, language, as a basic means of communication, their real fear is concerning the *fixation* of a few verbal statements as vessels of truth. Each man may formulate his creed — and tomorrow he should be such a new man as to need to tear it up. And even if the time-gap had not widened so much as to cause serious obsolescence, he would surely discount it by sighing, "But it doesn't quite catch the Reality whom I know."

Before going on to the last point of this paper I would point out the occurrence of spontaneous symbolic actions in a few of the first Publishers of Truth who felt called upon to go naked through the streets of a city as a sign of the inadequacy of any covering before the Lord. Into the use of *thee* and *thou* was packed the symbolism of belief in the equal dignity of all men — a symbolism now just reversed, a badge of separation and group consciousness, setting us *apart from* other men.

As such, the use of *thee* and *thou* ought to be dropped, but we suffer from the weakness with which we charge ritualists — the symbol has received rich historic incrustations of sentiment, and is retained after the vital life is gone. But the symbolism of *silence* is perennial and profound. For as into the divine Life one passes beyond words, beyond signs. Words, no matter how beautiful or sonorous, would be only blasphemous limitation upon that Reality. The most perfect description ceases to be a description and becomes silence. The most perfect prayer ceases to be verbalized prayer and becomes lived silence before Him. Silence before God is a dramatization of the *fullness of God* as we have found Him within ourselves.

But is there another *medium* of symbolic expression which Friends may use and do use freely and enthusiastically? It is the symbolism of *lived behaviors* and *vital concerns*. When one befriends a Negro one implicitly says, thereby, "I would that I might befriend all Negroes." That Negro stands for all Negroes, that man for *all* men. And that little act, that small segment of our behavior, is a gesture laden with *intention* for *all men* and *all* behavior. This little occasion, of befriending a fellow, has its earthly roots in a squalid tenement, but its head is crowned with Infinity. It is a fragment, in time, of my promptings from the side of the Eternal, and is an acted message to men.

Thus acts have a *double* meaning. The act of befriending had value for that Negro, and came to rest there. But, above that the act had *intentional reference* beyond that one case, and pointed out to *all men* and *all* acts and *all* life that is lived in the enfolding guidance of Creative Love.

When the American Friends Service Committee faces unemployment in the coal field it touches only a *few* people. They immediately receive the benefit. But over and above it is the intentional reference to *all*, and if sincerely done, it becomes a window of Divine Love. And the windows can be looked through, in both directions. And that is why such small undertakings as we make are important — far beyond their actual dimensions. They have an aura of the infinite about their heads. Viewed in the small, these undertakings are minute, against the world's sufferings, these little gestures of behavior and acted concern. But they are acted symbols, media of communication of the life of the Spirit, through Friends, and spoken to the world. They are lived words, spoken low and haltingly, but they must be spoken and the Spirit must give the increase — and fructify that infinity which is within them.

And that is why the effort of Friends to symbolize the Eternal in time, through acts and concerns, is an effective medium; *the symbol is a segment of life*, of the *divine Life*, and has within it all the flexibility and growth of Reality itself. Concerns that keep alive, grow and become *expanding* messages. The tension we saw arising between static word forms and the moving life of the Spirit does not arise here. The medium of symbolism and lived behavior is as dynamic and growing as the reality they symbolize. But the genius of this method requires that we be as ready to *drop* undertakings, when their message has been heard, as we are to *start* undertakings. Constant revision of our institutions, embodying acted messages and communications, is as necessary as constant revision of our personal creeds. The freeing, and making hallowed, through time, of *any* Quaker practice or institution is as dangerous as any other rigid symbol from which the life has departed — a dead, spent, burnt-out rocket that ought to be discarded.

Symbols, small in themselves, may point to the unspeakably great. A three-inch finger may point to the most distant star.

III

The Gathered Meeting

In the practice of group worship on the basis of silence come special times when the electric hush and solemnity and depth of power steals over the worshipers. A blanket of divine covering comes over the room, a stillness that can be felt is over all, and the worshipers are gathered into a unity and synthesis of life which is amazing indeed. A quickening Presence pervades us, breaking down some part of the special privacy and isolation of our individual lives and blending our spirits within a superindividual Life and Power. An objective, dynamic Presence enfolds us all, nourishes our souls, speaks glad, unutterable comfort within us, and quickens us in depths that had before been slumbering. The Burning Bush has been kindled in our midst, and we stand together on holy ground.

i

Such gathered meetings I take to be cases of group mysticism. It is commonly supposed that mystical experience is an individual affair, in which the lone soul is caught up into the first or second or third heaven and given to see things which it is not lawful for men to utter. And this, I presume, is most frequently the case. Furthermore, our current conception of the separateness of our various selves, of our self-containedness as individual centers of consciousness, would certainly favor the view that such depths of religious experience are individual, not capable of being shared by more than one person together with God.

But in mysticism we are in the realm of *experience*. Experience ought to speak first of all and not be blocked at the very beginning by a prior judgement of what is possible in the light of our *theories* of the nature of individuals. The actual should take precedence over our judgements of the possible. And if there are actually cases of group mysticism on hand, then the question as to whether they are possible is settled once and for all.

There are some cases recorded of two people sharing an experience of ascent together in the amazing Presence of God in His immediacy and glory. The most striking instance of which I know is that of St. Augustine and his mother, Monica. At Ostia, on the Tiber, soon after Augustine's final yielding to the inward persuasions of God within him, and as he and his mother were on their way back to Africa from Milan, they were together leaning in a window overlooking a garden and talking of the wonders of the life of dedicated souls. As they discoursed in intimacy they were together caught up into the sense of divine immediacy and given the bliss and rapture of the Touch of God.

"And when our discourse was brought to that point, that the very highest delight of the earthly sense, in the very purest material light, was, in the sweetness of that life, not only not worthy of comparison, but not even of mention; we raising up ourselves with a more glowing affection toward the 'Self-same,' did by degrees pass through all things bodily, even the very heaven, whence sun and moon and stars shine upon the earth; yea, we were soaring higher yet, by inward musing, and discourse and admiring of Thy works; and we came to our own minds, and went beyond them, that we might arrive at that region of never-failing plenty, where Thou feedest Israel forever with the food of truth, and where life is the Wisdom by whom all these things are made. ...And while we were discoursing and panting after her, we slightly touched on her with the whole effort of our heart; and we sighed, and there we have found the first fruits of the Spirit; and returned to vocal expressions of our mouths, where the word spoken has beginning and end" (*Confessions*, Book IX).

But we need not go to places remote in space and time to find similar experiences of joint elevation into the light of the Eternal Love. For today it occurs again and again that two or three individuals find the boundaries of their separateness partially melted down. It is not necessarily, or frequently, as exalted an experience as that of Augustine and Monica, nor does it involve losing touch with the world of sense. But after conversing together on central things of the spirit, two or more friends who know one another at deep levels find themselves wrapped in a sense of unity and of Presence such as quiets all words and enfolds them within an unspeakable calm and interknittedness within a vaster life. God's reality and His love become indubitable; His presence, like a living touch, is over them. As one friend speaks in such a silence, the words are found to join on closely to the thought of others, so that words become needless, and silence becomes a bridge, not of separation but of communication.

The gathered meeting I take to be of the same kind, still milder and more diffused, yet really of a piece with all mystical experience. For mystical times are capable of all gradings and shadings, from sublime heights to very mild moments of lift and very faint glimpses of glory. In the gathered meeting the sense is present that a new Life and Power has entered our midst. And we know not only that we stand erect in the holy Presence, but also that others sitting with us are experiencing the same exaltation and access of power. We may not know these our neighbors in any outwardly intimate sense, but we now know them, as it were, from within, and they know us in the same way, as souls now alive in the same areas and as blended into the body of Christ, which is His church. Again and again this community of life and guidance from the Presence in the midst is made clear by the way the spoken words uttered in the meeting join on to one another and to our inward thoughts. This, I presume, has been a frequent experience for us all, as a common life and current sweeps through all. We are in communication with one another because we are being communicated to, and through, by the Divine Presence. Such indeed is a taste of "the communion of saints."

John Hughes once told of two Friends sitting side by side in such a gathered meeting. The secret currents of worship flowed with power and then encountered a check. One man moved nervously but did not rise to his feet. Finally the other Friend arose and spoke a few words of searching power, and the meeting proceeded in a sense of covering. After the meeting had broken, the man who had spoken nudged his silent neighbor and said, "Next time, Henry, say it yourself."

But our interest in the gathered meeting is not in such striking side-phenomena as lift eyebrows of doubting Thomases, but in the central fact of the overshadowing presence of the Eternal One. For it is God Himself who graciously reveals Himself in such holy times. The gathered meeting, as group mysticism, shows all the four characteristics which William James applies to mystic states, namely, indescribability, a knowledge-quality, transiency, passivity.

The experience is ineffable, it is not completely describable in words. We live through such hours of expanded vision, yet never can we communicate to another all that wonder and power and life and recreation which we knew when swept along in the immediacy of the Divine Presence. To an absent friend we can only say what Philip said to Nathaniel concerning Jesus, "Come and see." And such must always be the report of any experience of God, by individuals or in groups. "He is wonder and joy, judgment and power. And He is *more* than all these. Come and see."

The experience has a knowledge-quality. The covering of God in the gathered meeting carries with it the sense of insight, of knowledge. We know Him as we have not known Him before. The secrets of this amazing world have been in some larger degree laid bare. We know life, and the world, and ourselves, from within, anew. And lo, there we have seen God. We may not issue from a gathered meeting a single crisp sentence or judgment of capsuled knowledge, yet we are infinitely more certain of the dynamic, living, working Life, for we have experienced a touch of that persuading Power that disquiets us until we find our home in Him. And, in the old phrases, we have directly known the healing which drops from beneath His wings. We have been re-energized with that Power and resensitized by that tenderness, to meet the daily world of men with new pangs and new steadiness.

It is transient. The sense of Divine covering in a group is rarely sustained more than three-quarters of an hour or an hour. One cannot seize hold upon it and restrain it from fading; or restore it the next Sunday at will. Each such meeting is a gracious gift of the Eternal Goodness, and the eyes of all must wait upon

Him who gives us meat in due season.

It carries a sense of passivity within it. We seem to be acted upon by a More-than-ourselves, who stills our time-torn spirits and breathes into us, as on Creation's day, the breath of life. When one rises to speak in such a meeting one has a sense of *being used*, of being played upon, of being spoken through. It is as amazing an experience as that of being *prayed through*, when we, the praying ones, are no longer the initiators of the supplication, but seem to be transmitters, who second an impulse welling up from the depths of the soul. In such an experience the brittle bounds of our selfhood seem softened and instead of saying, "I pray" or "He prays," it becomes better to say, "Prayer is taking place." So in a truly covered meeting an individual who speaks takes no credit to himself for the part he played in the unfolding of the worship. In fact he deeply regrets it if anyone, after the service, speaks in a complimentary fashion to *him*. For the feeling of being a pliant instrument of the Divine Will characterizes true speaking "in the life." Under such a covering an individual emerges into vocal utterance, frequently without fear and trembling, and subsides without self-consciousness into silence when his part is played. For one who is greater than all individuals has become the meeting place of the group, and He becomes the leader and director of worship. With wonder one hears the next speaker, if there be more, take up another aspect of the theme of the meeting. No jealousy, no regrets that *he* didn't think of saying that, but only gratitude that the angel has come and troubled the waters and that many are finding healing through the one Life. A gathered meeting is no place for the enhancement of private reputations, but for self-effacing and obedience to the whispers of the Leader.

A fifth trait of mystical experience may well be added to James' list — the sense of unity, unity with the Divine Life who has graciously allowed us to touch the hem of His garment, unity with our fellow worshipers, for He has broken down the middle wall of partition between our separate personalities and has flooded us with a sense of *fellowship.* This unity with our fellow worshipers, such that we are "written in one another's hearts," is in one sense created and instituted in the hour of worship. But in a deeper sense it is *discovered* in that hour that we *are* together in one body, which is the true and Catholic church invisible. And in a fashion the vividness of our unity fades, is transient, grows weaker after the rise of the meeting. But the fact *disclosed* in the meeting, namely, that we *are* one body, hid with Christ in God, remains, secure from the ebb and flow of *feelings* and *emotion.*

Recall the counsel of George Fox, "But all Friends, mind that which is eternal, which gathers your hearts together up to the Lord, and lets you see that ye are written in one another's heart" (Selections from *Epistles,* page 22). And Isaac Penington queries, "Are ye truly united, so as to become one Spirit with the Lord? Are all the walls of partition broken down? And is there nothing now between you, but of two ye are made one in that which uniteth?" (*Works* II, 70).

ii

What is the ground and foundation of the gathered meeting? In the last analysis, it is, I am convinced, the Real Presence of God.

It is easy to call this sense of covering a mere psychological phenomenon. Psychological notions have so permeated our contemporary thinking that it is very easy to rush hastily to popular concepts, lying ready at hand, and apply them to all experience. In one sense *all* that we think and experience is "merely a psychological phenomenon." Our experiences of beauty are all "psychological." Political ideas and events are "psychological," for they are apprehended in minds. Strictly, one might try to say that all of history, as intelligible accounts of the past, is "psychological." Even natural sciences are "psychological," for they are constructions in and of human minds. One might even go so far as to say that mathematical thinking is "psychological." This tendency to read everything in terms of psychological and clap immediately upon all things experienced the badge and label of subjectivity, is called by the technical German word *Psychologismus.* And on this platform of *Psychologismus* all of religious experience becomes "merely psychological," and presumably, merely subjective.

Not only would mysticism lose its claim to be substantially real, resting not upon subjective changes in the human person, but upon the real activity of an existent, self-revealing God, but also prayer, praise, thanksgiving, sin, forgiveness would all become "merely psychological," merely subjective.

Against the devastating implications of *Psychologismus* there has been, in the last three decades, a sharp rebellion in favor of *realism.* Knowledge of all kinds, realism claims, is not merely subjective, it attains the real. The mere fact that knowledge is entertained in our minds does not create a presumption of falsity, or of lack of fidelity to the real. But in such a return to realism we are opening the gates again to the contention of the mystics, that mystical experience is not merely a matter of subjective states but a matter of objective reality.

I believe that the group mysticism of the gathered meeting rests upon the Real Presence of God in our midst. Quakers generally hold to a belief in Real Presence, as firm and solid as the belief of Roman Catholics in the Real Presence in the host, the bread and the wine of the Mass. In the host the Roman Catholic is convinced that the literal, substantial Body of Christ is present. For him the Mass is not a mere symbol, a dramatizing of some figurative relationship of man to God. It rests upon the persuasion that an Existence, a Life, the Body of Christ, is really present and entering into the body of man. Here the Quaker is very near the Roman Catholic. For the Real Presence of the gathered meeting is an existential fact. To use philosophical language, it is an ontological matter, not merely a psychological matter. The bond of union in divine fellowship is existential and real, not figurative. It is the life of God Himself, within whose life we live and move and have our being. And the gathered meeting is a special case of holy fellowship of the blessed community.

iii

What conditions favor a gathered meeting? Even to ask this question is to speak like a Western man who wants to capture the law regulating the occurrence, in order that he may capture and institute the occurrence itself at will. But in another sense it is not a Western man's question, for the mystics of the East have also anxiously watched the conditions which facilitate the dawning of the Vision Splendid. For example, all Yogic practices are purgative disciplines of body and mind which, it is hoped, will make more likely the occurrence of the Divine Experience. And the medieval mystics sought to discern rungs of the ladder whereby they might climb upward toward the Celestial Vision — *cogitatio, meditatio, contemplatio.*

But all this stands in opposition to another fundamental element in religion, the principle of submission (Islam, if we think of Mohammedanism). For the center of the religious attitude is submission, not control. Submit yourselves to God, do not seek to bend Him to your will, or use Him at your convenience. It is not religion, but magic, which tries to find the compelling formula, the abracadabra which makes the gods our slaves. But over against the incantation of the medicine man stands the prayer of the truly religious man. And prayer is shown in its final attitude, as is so frequently said, in the words of Jesus, "Nevertheless not my will but Thine be done." The special visitations of God, in individual and in group mysticism, are, in the last analysis, the free gift of God's gracious love, freely given.

Let us therefore venture upon the question of the conditions favoring a gathered meeting in an attitude of humility, not in the spirit of the masterly man, so characteristic of our modern post-Baconian age. We seek at best to discern merely favoring conditions and releasing stimuli, not the full control of the event.

One condition for such a group experience seems to be this: *Some* individuals need already, upon entering the meeting, to be gathered deep in the spirit of worship. There must be some kindled hearts when the meeting begins. In them, and from them, begins the *work* of worship. The spiritual devotion of a few persons, silently deep in active adoration, is needed to kindle the rest, to help those others who enter the service with tangled, harried, distraught thoughts to be melted and quieted and released and made pliant, ready for the work of God and His Real Presence.

This is a purely invisible work. It is not done through wearing on one's face a look of rapt contemplation such that others in the room, seeing the face, will be stimulated to a like contemplation. Such external stimuli are accidental. They might aid a few; they would certainly repel many more. But there is a real invisible work of kindling and of mutual assistance in worship which some of the worshipers must do, directing it upon others along with themselves. It is an internal work of prayer. Its language is not "I," or "You," but "We." It is an awakening and an attuning that goes on with energy in the soul. In power and labor one lifts the group, in inward prayer, high before the throne. With work of soul the kindled praying worshiper holds the group, his comrades and himself, high above the sordid and trivial, and prays in quiet, offering that Light may drive away the shadows of self-will. Where this inward work of upholding prayer is wholly absent, I am not sure that a gathered meeting is at all likely to follow.

This means a preceding preparation for worship. Worship, and preparation for worship, begin before one has left one's home. They begin when one wakes up on Sunday morning, before one has got out of bed. Worship in a meeting-house with one's friends should be only a special period of a life of worship that underlies all one's daily affairs. For he who carries a Shekinah daily in his heart, and practices continual retirement within the Shekinah, *at the same time as he is carrying on his daily affairs*, has begun to prepare for worship, for he has never ceased worshipping. Such worship is no intermittent process, but a foundation layer of the life of the children of the kingdom. And such a special sense of bondedness and unity with others as is experienced in the gathered meeting is only a time of particular enhancement of the life of bondedness and fellowship in love among souls which is experienced daily, as we carry one another in inward upholding prayer.

A second condition concerns the spoken words of the meeting. Certainly the deepness of the covering of a meeting is not proportional to the number of words spoken. A gathered meeting may proceed entirely in silence, rolling on with increasing depth and intensity until the meeting breaks and tears are furtively brushed away. Such really powerful hours of unbroken silence frequently carry a genuine progression of spiritual change and experience. They are *filled* moments, and the quality of the second fifteen minutes is definitely different from the quality of the first fifteen minutes. Outwardly, all silences seem alike, as all minutes are alike by the clock. But inwardly the Divine Leader of worship directs us through progressive unfoldings of ministration, and may in silence bring an inward climax which is as definite as the climax of the Mass, when the host is elevated in adoration.

But more frequently some words are spoken. I have in mind those meeting hours which are not dominated by a single sermon, a single twenty-minute address, well-rounded out, with all the edges tucked in so there is nothing more to say. In some of our meetings we may have too many polished examples of homiletic perfection which lead the rest to sit back and admire but which close the question considered, rather than open it. Participants are converted into spectators; active worship on the part of all drifts into passive reception of external instruction. To be sure, there are gathered meetings which arise about a single towering mountain peak of a sermon. One kindled soul may be the agent whereby the slumbering embers within are quickened into a living flame.

But I have more particularly in mind those hours of worship in which no one person, no one speech, stands out as the one that "made" the meeting, those hours wherein the personalities that take part verbally are not enhanced as individuals in the eyes of others, but are subdued and softened and lost sight of because, in the language of Fox, "The Lord's Power was over all." Brevity, earnestness, sincerity — and frequently a lack of polish — characterized the best Quaker speaking. The words should rise like a shaggy crag upthrust from the surface of silence under the pressure of river power and yearning, contrition, and wonder. But on the other hand the words should not rise up like a shaggy crag. They should not break the silence, but continue it. For the Divine Life who is ministering through the medium of silence is the same Life as is now ministering through words. And when such words are truly spoken "in the Life," then when such words cease, the *uninterrupted* silence and worship continue, for silence and words have been of one texture, one piece. Second and third speakers only continue the enhancement of the moving Presence, until a climax is reached, and the discerning head of the meeting knows when to break it.

A recent book discussed use of silences. The artistic skill with which his characters speak through pauses and omissions and unspoken words is striking. The vocal power of silence in music is widely known. Rests, silences can be as expressive in a symphony as is a crash of sound. In a truly gathered meeting, restraint in one's utterances is often more releasing than are multiplied words. Words that hint at the wonder of God, but that do not attempt to exhaust it, have an open-ended character. In the silences of our hearts the Holy Presence completes the unfinished words far more satisfyingly.

The themes made central in truly gathered meetings are infinite. But one might venture to raise the question whether some types of themes are more congruous with such a meeting than others. Some text that suddenly recalls the eternal, abiding central relation of Man and God seems particularly apt to serve as a releasing stimulus, but by no means as *compelling* the arrival of the covering. Such a passage as "Lord, thou hast been our dwelling place in all generations" opens up a vista of gargantuan yet delicate proportions. "Deep calleth unto deep at the noise of thy waterspouts; all thy waves and thy billows are gone over me."

But humble, personal, daily incidents, or wisps of openings that have dawned with vividness in some quiet soul, or the tragic-heroic turmoil of events of the day, met in the frame of the Eternal Patience and Persuasion may equally serve as themes within such a meeting.

Vocal prayer, poured out from a humble heart, frequently shifts a meeting from a heady level of discussion to the deeps of worship. Such prayers serve as an unintended rebuke to our shallowness and drive us deeper into worship, and commitment. They open the gates of devotion, adoration, submission, confession. They help to unite the group at the level at which real unity is sought. For unity in the springs of life's motivations is far more significant than unity in phrases or outward manners. Such prayers not only "create" that unity; they also give voice to it, and the worshipers are united in a silent amen of gratitude.

iv

But what if the meeting has not been a gathered meeting? Are those meetings failures that have not been hushed by a covering? Quite definitely they are not. *If we have been faithful*, we may go home content and nourished from any meeting.

Let us be quite clear that mystical exaltation is not essential to religious dedication and to every occurrence of religious worship. Many a man professes to be without a shred of mystical elevation, yet is fundamentally a heaven-dedicated soul. It would be a tragic mistake to suppose that religion is only for a small group, who have certain vivid but transient inner experiences, and to preach those experiences so that those who are relatively insensitive to them should feel excluded, denied access to the Eternal Love, deprived of a basic necessity for religious living. The crux of religious living lies in the *will*, not in transient and variable states. Utter dedication of the will to God is open to *all*, for every man can will, and can will his will into the will of God. Where the will to will God's will is present, there is a child of God. When there are graciously given to us such glimpses of glory as aid us in softening [our] own will, then we may be humbly grateful. But glad willing away of self, that the will of God, so far as it can be discerned, may become what we will — that is the basic condition.

And as individual mystics who are led deep into the heart of devotion learn to be weaned away from reliance upon special vision, learn not to clamor perpetually for the heights but to walk in shadows and valleys, dry places, for months and years together, so must group worshipers learn that worship is fully valid when there are no thrills, no special sense of covering, but chiefly valleys and dry places. Misunderstandings, heartaches, questionings, have been caused by excessive demand for special experiences, for their enjoyment and for their prolongation. But I am persuaded that a deeper sifting of religion leads us down to the will, steadfastly oriented toward the will of God. In that steadiness of will one walks serene and unperturbed, praying only "Thy will be done," confident that we are in His hands and He educates us in ways that we do not expect, but by means of dryness as well as by means of glory, we walk in gratitude if His sun shines upon us, and in serenity if He leads us in valleys and dry places. Then we have learned the secret of how to abound and how to be in want. For the life in which I have died and is hid with Christ in God so that the I is a new and a recreated and triumphant self — that life is an enduring life, immersed in Eternity, and not varying with transient states.

Like the individual soul, the group must learn to endure spiritual weather without dismay. Some hours of worship are full of glow and life, but others lack the quality. The disciplined soul, and the disciplined group, have learned to cling to the reality of God's presence, whether the feeling of presence is great or faint. If only the group has been knit about the very springs of motivation, the fountain of the will, then real worship has taken place. If the wind of the Spirit, blowing whither He wills, warms the group into an inexpressible sense of unity, then the worshipers are profoundly grateful. If no blanket of divine covering is warmly felt, and *if the wills have been offered together in the silent work of worship*, worshipers may go home content and nourished, and say, "It was a good meeting." In the venture of group worship, souls must learn to accept spiritual "weather" and go deeper, in will, into Him who makes all things beautiful in their time.

IV

The Publishers of Truth

The apostolic church of the Spirit can spring up again, today, in these troubled times. The fires burn low, but they can be kindled again, if we be kindled. Do we really understand the message of George Fox and the first generation of Friends? Are we really persuaded that the days of revelation and of amazing power can come upon us, that Christendom can know a new birth of life and light? The twilight of the earthly gods is settling upon us, but no historical necessity dooms us to decades of night before the day star can arise within us, and within the social fabric.

Four fabrics, at least, must converge, however, if such a profound awakening of spiritual religion is to take place. The basic condition is the soul-shaking discovery that God Himself is active, is dynamic, is here, is brooding over us all, is prompting and instructing us within, in amazing immediacy. This is not something to believe, it is something to experience, in the solemn, sacred depths of our beings. When we so find Him — something of the conquering, blinding vision of the Nazarene becomes ours. The water of the very commonplace human nature can be changed into the wine of the Spirit. No calculation of the chances of success in a commercial, war-scarred world is complete, if He be not considered. No weighing of God's power against the lethargy of the church can prove that He must wait a better day. This is the first condition — firsthand and vivid awareness of the victorious, persuading power of the Spirit.

The second factor is our answering dedication. The natural response of the soul to God is absolute and complete surrender to Him. Too many mental reservations, too many cautions of worldly prudence, and we become disobedient to the heavenly vision, and the apostolic fires are quenched, or smolder as a feeble flame. *Fearing excess we have not feared caution,* or dared to believe that the only security is in Him. When Francis of Assisi stripped himself of his last garment and proclaimed that henceforth he would only know his father to be the Father in Heaven, he knew the complete release of dedication. Such dedication is imperative.

I believe that a band of kindled and dedicated preachers can arise who can shake the countryside for ten miles around, and in this day become a second band of Publishers of Truth and release the hopes of thousands for the church of the Spirit. But they must be blinded souls — blinded by the splendor of God so that discouragement and apathy and mediocrity and selfishness in our meetings and in our churches and in our world will not dismay them. And they must be utterly dedicated souls who have, so far as they know how, completely committed themselves, their powers and their future, to the Inner Keeper. Their dedication must be as complete and irrevocable as that of monks who take life-vows. They live in no outward cells, but within them is the Shekinah, the Holy of Holies where they listen in wonder and joy to the breathings of the Inner Voice. Such preaching bands will call other men to listen to the same Inner Teacher, until the church and the Society of Friends become a listening body of heaven-instructed souls.

A third condition is that individuals who have been given such a vision may find one another, be aware that others exist who share the dream and the call with them. Here and there throughout the land are solitary souls who burn in hope for a profound recovery of the religion of the Spirit. They know in themselves the quickening fires, but like separately burning sticks they need some *togetherness* for the fire to burn with its hottest flame. It is not organization that they need, but fellowship, the opportunity to know one another in that which is eternal. A common understanding, a common sense of mission, a common Life and Love and happy enthrallment furnish the matrix out of which epoch-shaking rediscovery of living religion can grow. The Wider Quaker Fellowship furnished thin bonds of such togetherness. But something vastly closer is needed before these, and many, many more, in our Society and out, in the church and out, become self-starting, God-started Publishers of Truth. The American Friends Fellowship Council may be the agency through which such togetherness in the quickening fires is mediated. But organizational structures such as the Fellowship Council can only channel and make articulate the living Life of the Spirit as He moves actively in quickening men and women. The dynamic is within the soul. But message-bearing individuals and bands can arise today — quickening lives and lips touched with coals from the altar. Inhibiting fears of proselytizing have no place. They have place only if the effort is to win recruits to an earthly *organization*. But if the message is for all kinds and conditions of men, to open the foundations of God in the heart, and to walk in humble dedication in the direct love of the Nazarene, then all such inhibitions fade away. Message-bearing should be the function of all kindled souls, message-bearing through lip as well as through life and active service. For there will always be a place for the foolishness of preaching.

A fourth condition for a spiritual awakening is "the fullness of time." Is today such an age? Or do war and turmoil distract men's minds too hopelessly? I believe we live in a waiting age, when multitudes are convinced that something vastly deeper than they know in the present church is fundamentally needed. The land is full of seekers, the church is full of seekers, the Society of Friends has its full share of seekers after genuineness and vitality and integrity at the base of life which they have not yet seen illustrated widely. Such discontent is due not to weakness but to vision. Over the horizon men dimly see something glorious, they know not what. But what they see is Christ walking again in lowly, simple love, recapturing the church and world for Himself, rebuking the scribes and the Pharisees who sit in Moses' seat, tenderly leading men to share in His immediacy and enthrallment in God. They know something far more glorious is meant by Christian discipleship than the half-hearted loyalties of the day have shown them. The Inner Teacher is already at work within them. If Publishers of Truth will arise, fired with a genuineness and a simple directness that can only come in Spirit-taught and God-humbled souls, their words will run like fire through dry grass.

Yes, the times are ripe for an escape from Quietism in the realm of preaching, as we have already escaped from Quietism in the realm of public service. The four conditions are fulfilled today. Hear the words of George Fox and recover the expectant, outreaching, universal spirit from which they issued: "Sound, sound abroad, you faithful servants of the Lord and witnesses in His name... and prophets of the Highest, and angels of the Lord! Sound ye all abroad in the world, to the awakening and raising of the dead, that they may be awakened, and raised up out of the grave, to hear the voice that is living. For the dead have long heard the dead, and the blind have long wandered among the blind, and deaf among the deaf. Therefore sound, sound, ye servants and prophets and angels of the Lord."

PART THREE

Room for the Infinite

Four rather different pieces are included in this part.

"Room for the Infinite" was written in early 1937. It reflects Thomas Kelly's keen interest in Oriental thought and his work on Emile Myerson. It is a significant foreshadowing of the spiritual upheaval he experienced a few months later. It was published in The Friend, *June 17, 1937*.

"Secret Seekers" is taken from the manuscript of an address to an unidentified Quaker group, probably in the latter part of 1940, and printed in Motive.

In the summer of 1939, Thomas Kelly visited an Episcopal monastery, The Society of St. John the Evangelist, in Cambridge, Massachusetts. While there, he wrote these "Reflections."

"Hasten unto God" is taken from the manuscript of an address to Friends in Lansdowne, Pennsylvania. The probable date is fall of 1938.

I

Room for the Infinite

Chinese landscape paintings frequently puzzle Western observers. They seem to be so bare, so simple. A jutting crag, a tumbling waterfall, a brook flowing out of illimitable distance, a moving tree overhanging the brook. And between and around the objects lie vast spaces, unbroken stretches of uniform background out from which these few powerful hills, or singing brooks, or rhythm-filled trees project. Can it be that the Chinese artists have only rudimentary skill and artistic sense and can proceed no further in their paintings? Did they not know how to fill the surface to the full? Yet critics tell us they are the world's masters of landscape.

There is a profundity and subtlety in such pictures that we never should have missed. Such painting carries the universe in its bosom. It sets forth the Infinite, the Everlasting Background and Source of all things, and shows us the infinite particulars as outjutting revelations of Itself. Out from It they came, back into It they retire. There is no disconnection; the finite is a fragmentary disclosure of the Infinite, a rhythm-filled continuation of that unspeakably full Life which gives it birth.

112

There is no barrenness in the picture. For those open spaces are the *fullest* part of the scene. Space surrounds and embraces the rock and wind-moved trees in its tender, mighty clasp. It extends behind all objects as their common background. All spaces are one Space. All things have a final Environment and Mother. Sit before a painting of a few bamboos, a few joints that are resolved, here and there, out of the undifferentiated background. It is enough; one worships; one cannot ask for more.

For the open spaces are the analogue of the silences in a meeting for worship. Too full for articulate expression, the glory and fullness of the Infinite can only be portrayed by the unbroken silence. Unhurried, unharried, we feel our way back to the world's Mother, as the child feels its way to its parent's arms. And there the Unspeakable is enough, fuller than expostulations and assurances. Yet again and again from out of that background emerge words, outthrusts of the Divine Life, a few sentences uttered in time yet pronounced from Eternity, a daily matter is set in cosmic frame. Resumption of silence is but the continuation of silence; unbroken space extends behind crag and cascade and river. To crowd the canvas full with finite figures — that were a calamity indeed, that would be to miss the most important part of the picture.

We live in a secularized culture. And what does that mean? It means that we do crowd the canvas full. We leave no room for the Infinite. The daily affairs are — just the daily affairs. No awareness of the background of the Infinite Life, outthrusting, inbreathing, self-revealing, sets off the day's experience and gives it cosmic sweep and dignity. The primrose by the river's bank is — but a primrose. There is no room for wonder, for glory, for worship in the secular mind. A spade is a spade, a saint is a collection of atoms, the Cross is made of cellulose.

The secular mind of our day lacks depth, it lacks that dimension whereby the finite is bound to the Infinite. We crowd the canvas full. We must keep the radio going, or hurry away to the movies, or the next committee, or hunt for conversation, or fidget till we find three more for bridge. Laurence Binyon, in his *Spirit of Man in Asian Art*, says we Westerners are afraid of space, of all-filling, all-embracing space. Awful, awe-inspiring, it engulfs us all. But we dare not become aware of it. We cover it over with the near, the local, the detailed. And, filling the canvas with such, we say there is no Infinite Background, when we have blotted it out. The secular mind is too much ours, as individuals, as a culture.

But now and again one finds a life so lived that its daily deeds are set in a frame of Eternity. There is a spaciousness about such a life. Majestic space is its aura. Unhurried and sure, it breathes forth out of the Everlasting. The odor of the Ageless is upon it. By its serenity we are shamed and recalled. Shuddering and quieted we turn again Home.

Like personality ringed by Eternity, Quaker

worship has gigantic meaning. Like the Chinese landscape it portrays the Infinite and its relation to the finite, the Unspoken and Unspeakable and its relation to the spoken and the thought. It is an acted drama of the true nature of things, of man and God. It is the antithesis of the secular mind. It holds the secret of Reality in itself, that secret after which a semidiscontented, semidisillusioned secularity is seeking, yet knows not what it seeks. For it restores wonder, glory, radiance, worship, the deepest responses of men to the deepest secrets of God and of His world.

II

Secret Seekers

We know that Quakerism arose in a time when England was full of seekers, men and women who hungered desperately for the last deeps of reality, for Him whom their souls craved more than life itself. And we are apt to sigh and say, "Oh, that men hungered today for God, as they did two hundred and fifty years ago. But now men don't want God; they want automobiles and financial security and social recognition. They don't want God."

But I submit that there are as many *secret seekers* today as there were in the days of Fox, men and women and boys and girls who have a *deep, deep* hunger for the last Eternal Ground of their lives. For all of us have our moments of absolute honesty within ourselves, when we *know* that these customary securities and goals for which we seem to be living are not our *final* and *real destiny*. In these moments of honesty we are disillusioned about all these earthly quests. A deep-throated bell, muffled or clear, comes ringing in the ears of our souls from a distant shore in Eternity and awakens in us a vague uneasiness, a homesickness, a longing. We've all heard that bell, distant or clear, calling us to a vaster life. Like a wild duck who has paused to pick at the straws of a barnyard, but who finds a dim stirring, a homing instinct which makes him leave the sticks and straws and easy comfortable food for the body, and wing his way into the blue south sky, where lies his home, so do you and I have a voice within us, a homing instinct of the soul which whispers within us uneasiness and urgency, and the call of Eternity for our souls. We are all seekers, for we feel that we are *sought.*

Nor does the clamor and confusion of war days drown out this deep, deep hunger of the soul to be grounded upon whatever Eternal Verity there be that undergirds our human existence. Rather, war days only show us more vividly how falsely we have lived, at secondary levels, for secondary goals, for transient securities. Multitudes of people, and you in this room are among them, are groping down deeper and deeper for the last bedrock, unshakable Verity of human existence, in order that there, if haply they find that Eternal Rock, they may build upon It the mansion of their souls. As I traveled widely in Germany two years ago, I found men asking not merely for physical relief and escape from persecution by emigration, but for the deeps of experience of a life that is hid with Christ, with God. The hunger of the world which we as a Religious Society have to consider is not merely the physical hunger of the refugees, important as that is. We must face the spiritual hunger of a generation that is desperately concerned for realities, desperately discontented with shams in the profoundest area of the soul's life. For today, here in America, and here in this meeting, and here in your meeting on Sunday morning, are *seekers*. War doesn't stop this seeking of the soul after God; it only sharpens and accelerates it, for many. And to this seeking for the deeps, to this perennial God-hunger of the human soul, we must be ministering, and not stop short at physical relief. Until we are doing this, here in this meeting, and throughout the world, the hungry sheep look up and are not fed.

To you in this room who are seekers, to you, young and old who have toiled all night and caught nothing, but who want to launch out into deeps and let down your nets for a draught, I want to speak, as simply, as tenderly, as clearly as I can. For God *can* be found. There *is* a last Rock for your souls, a resting place of absolute peace and joy and power and radiance and security. There is a Divine Center into which your life can slip, a new and absolute orientation to God, a Center where you live with Him, and out from which you see all of life, through new and radiant vision tinged with new sorrows and pangs, new joys unspeakable and full of glory.

Someone has said of St. Francis that when a young man, as other young men run away to see the world, so he ran away to God. But how can we run away to God? What direction shall we run?

A few weeks ago a young college man, an athlete, sat in my office and we talked of this amazing Center, this life that is hid with Christ in God. And as I tried to tell him something of what God in His graciousness had shown of Himself to

me, he said, "Gee, I'd like to find a God like that!"
And I thought I almost heard the words of Job,
speaking of behalf of mankind, "O that I knew
where I might find him."

What direction shall we run, if we would run
away to God? I can only answer, He is *within* you
already. Seek Him in the very deeps of your
souls. But you say, "I thought we were to seek Him
in the Bible." I should reply, He is not in the Bible, as such. For the Bible, as such, is a book,
and words; and what you want is not a book but a
living God; not words, but the *Word*, the Living
Word. It is not the words of a book, but the Living
Word who animated and owned those writers who
wrote the Bible, that we crave. "As the hart panteth after the water brooks, so panteth my soul after thee, O God." The Book points beyond itself,
to Him who has been found by its writers. And because He is already in the deeps of your own
souls, these words of the Bible are made living
and vivid to you. Read your Bibles, but *that isn't
being religious*. Read your Bibles, and feel your
way back into that Source and Spring of Life which
bubbled up in the Bible-writers. And you'll find
that Source and Spring of Life bubbling up *within
you also*. And you'll find yourself in deep fellowship with these writers, because your life and
theirs go back into the same Living Spring. It is as
Robert Barclay says. The Scriptures are not the
Fountain, but a declaration of the Fountain. And
it is into that Fountain itself that we would step,
when the angel troubles the waters, and be heal-
ed.

What direction shall we run, if we would run away to God? Some of you may say, "I shall seek Him in nature, in its beauty and its power, in its storm-tossed fury and the quiet of the forests and golden glow of sunsets." And I should reply, Yes, He comes upon us many times, in these settings, on a mountain top, at twilight, and His Presence seems very real, in those precious moments. But He is *more* than nature. And He whom we find in Nature is He who is behind and beneath and *upholding* nature. And remember, we are part of that Nature, and He is equally behind and beneath and upholding us, as well as the mountains and the stars. We are led back behind nature to the Source and Fountain of Nature, welling up *within* us, welling up *beyond* us in the sunset. And it is because He is within us that Nature *beyond* us is revealed as a companion of our inner souls. For we and Nature go back into the same creative Life. Immediacy, vivid immediacy in that Life of the Universe, is what we seek. Not in the earthquake, not in the whirlwind, not in the fire, but in a still small voice that we all have heard within us is He most immediately to be found.

What direction shall we run, if we would run away to God? Some of you may say, "I shall go into the city slums, into the war-stricken areas, into work with sharecroppers and dispossessed miners. And in the world's sufferings I shall find God." And I would reply, Yes, many have found Him in these settings and scenes of squalor and tragedy. But He whom you seek *is already there in the midst of the suffering*, bearing its load, before you ever became a bearer of the world's suffering. It is because He was already speaking within you that you went to share the burden.

It is this Inner Witness, this Inner Light, that grows brighter, in fellowship with Scripture writers, in fellowship with nature, in fellowship with service and suffering.

And now I want to let you in on a secret. How can you be sure there is a God to be found at the other end of the search? Because He has *already* been showing Himself to you, in your very impulse to seek Him. Did *you* start the search for Him? *He started you* on the search for Him, and lovingly, anxiously, tenderly guides you to Himself. You knock on heaven's gate, because He has already been standing at the door and knocking within you, disquieting you and calling you to arise and seek your Father's house. It is as St. Augustine says: He was within, and we mistakenly sought Him without. Within us all is a slumbering miracle, a latent Christ, a Light, a Power, an immediacy with God. To find this "indwelling Christ" actively, dynamically working within us, is to find the secret that Jesus wanted to give to men. It isn't a matter of *believing* in the Inner Light, it is a matter of *yielding* your lives to Him. It is a matter of daily, hourly going down into the Shekinah of the soul, in the silence, finding yourselves continually recreated, and realigned and corrected again and again from warping effects of outer affairs. It is having a *Center* of creative power and joy and peace and creation within you.

III

Reflections

Now there were shepherds in a certain country, abiding in the field, keeping watch by night over their flock.

In the morning, when they returned to their homes, the wife of one said, "How has the night gone? What has thou seen?" To which the shepherd replied, "In the night a lamb was born, in the depths of whose eyes I saw the matchless glory of heaven."

The other shepherd likewise returned to his home in the morning. "How has the night gone?" asked the wife. He answered, "By spring we shall have a large herd. Then canst thou have many things."

A little child was born — in Bethlehem, or somewhere else. It matters not the place.

The Guide and I stood watching and adoring.

"Look! What is it they are doing with yonder cradle? Are they not shaping it into a cross?"

The Guide replied, "No, look again. You have reversed the meaning. Out of the cross they are making a cradle."

I saw a man who bowed in reverent admiration

before the wonders of a stone.

The stone sought to bow in reverent admiration before the man. But it could not.

Therein lies the glory and the greatness of man.

The Guide led me high above the earth, up to the spaces between the swinging stars. Beneath us, far below, lay the earth, wrapped in the black garment of night. As we watched, a shimmering, silvery mist rose slowly from the earth and enveloped it in a faint veil of light. Slowly, slowly, the silver mist was suffused with pink, then deeper red, then crimson, till at last the earth was a ball of blazing light.

I watched in dumb amazement at the wonder, and at last: "What is it yonder that happens on the earth?"

To which the Guide replied, "The day is dawning on the earth."

"But what is the silver which enfolds it, and the crimson red which illumines it?"

"These," said the Guide, "are the tears of men, and their blood."

And I replied, "Then indeed truly is the day dawning on the earth."

These lines are written in a monastery, in a cell of devotion. Outside the shadows of the evening are falling upon the quiet, friendly garden where a few moments ago three of us, two Fathers of the Catholic tradition and a Friend, were speaking of the sacraments. There was much talk of the "covenanted channels," of the seven to which Catholics hold, of the two which Protestants practice. So long as questions of theological mathematics were upper, of seven or of two, there was a danger which we tacitly avoided. It became evident that I, an "unbaptized" Quaker, was not a Christian, except for the saving provision which allowed one to be a "Christian by desire."

Yet as the conversation moved to the love of God, to the need of Christ being formed in us, to the outgoing love of the Nazarene, to the blind and lame and wounded in body and soul in these days, the conversation became a sacrament where the Presence was as truly in our midst as He is in the Mass within the chapel walls. For the time being, Sacramentalist and Quaker were one, in the fellowship of the Church Universal.

These days have been rich in such fellowship. The simple meals in the refectory, in complete silence, accompanied throughout by reading of Psalms or the *Imitation of Christ* or the lives of the saints have been at times sacraments indeed. A few words spoken in a darkened hallway have been shadowed over by the Holy One.

But outside are the homes of friends, where, behind the raveling cares and toil of the day, men and women and little children grow daily more strong in the bonds of love. Some hundreds of miles away are college men in work camps of Service Committee who will surely find, through simple labor for others, new outlines of the face of Christ, new vistas of the Kingdom. To the west an aged friend of eighty years smiles peacefully between earth and heaven, a benediction to those who pause and grow sensitive to the glimmerings of sainthood in their midst. Downstairs lies a sick priest, triumphant in the sacrament of pain. Across the waters to the east lies Europe, at this hour sleeping fitfully in the fear of war yet filled with...

Yes, outside are ugly factories and scheming merchants and tawdry roadhouses...

Now the bell for compline rings and I shall go into the chapel and kneel with my black-robed fellow Christians in the adoration of Him who would draw all men unto Himself and touch all of life with His Glory.

IV

Hasten unto God

You and I are here this evening to go as deeply as we possibly can into the last, last depth and ground of human life, and into its outworking in a heaven-led, God-directed mode of being. This is not a trifling undertaking. We dare not be perfunctory and just fill up an evening with sweet platitudinous breathings. It is an imperative necessity that we do this. The world, by its chaos, shows that we humans have been building our houses upon the sand. *Where and what is the Rock, and am I built upon it?* The church by its weakness and supine worldliness, shows desperate need of its radical reorientation, and fundamentally its rediscovery that religion is *primarily* built around God, joy in God, fellowship and love and victory and peace in God, not around the world; and that salvation is built, not upon forums for discussion of public affairs, but upon blood. By blood I mean not *theological* blood, but human-divine blood, yours and mine, poured out in self-forgetful consecration to God's renovation of a world in unspeakable need and suffering and darkness of vision.

We must go down to the bottom, and find the

Rock. Let us try, tonight, with terrible earnestness, to face the depth and glimpse some of the heights of religion in ourselves, as individuals, for the meek and mild mediocrity of most of us, stands in sharp contrast to that volcanic, upheaving, shaggy power of the prophets, whose descendants we were meant to be. And our paled-out love for one another and for all men is a feeble shadow of that blinding, wooing, winning, overcoming love of Jesus of Nazareth, whose name we have dared to take on our lips. And our immersion in the world's suffering is like tickling our toes in the ocean of sorrow and need, in comparison with that Calvary-life which plunges into the whole flood, or in comparison with that spirit that draws the spears of the world into its bosom.

i

The times are severe, the need is great, and we must *hasten*: we all agree. But whither shall we hasten? Two directions we must hasten, in order to plumb the depths and scale the heights of life. We must *hasten unto God*; and we must *hasten into the world*. But the first is the prime need; though the world be aflame by its own blindness and hate, and narrow ideals. We must first *hasten unto God*. Men whose heads have not rested in the bosom of God are not yet ready to be saviors of the world.

This may sound platitudinous. But it is preached all too little. The center of religion is in a living, vital, unspeakably intimate fellowship of the soul with God, wherein we sing and dance and leap for joy in His Presence. And some of us have found that life, that overturning, realigning experience of Him in His immediacy, and we walk in joy and power. But some have, I fear, never even guessed that there *is* possible such a life with God as makes all creation new—although the words have fallen on our ears since childhood. Even the Quaker preaching upon the *immediacy* of Divine Presence, for which there is no substitute in religious learnedness or endeavor, even this preaching has been a thing for many Quakers to *believe in*, not a gateway into the experience of God Himself. I say this pointedly and without apology. For if we knew Him and His Power and Glory in full immediacy and walked daily in humility and erectness of soul, such resplendent gleams of divine light and glory would shine out from us as would kindle other lives into a heavenly flame, and we should shake the countryside for ten miles around.

Hasten unto God. Why? Not because we ought to. Fellowship with God isn't a bitter duty. Fellowship with God is the deepest joy of human existence. It is the Pearl of Great Price, for which we should sell all we have, and in joy, purchase the pearl. We haven't gotten down to bottom until we have been down to God in the base of our souls at rest in Him. We are not our truest, deepest selves until we are selves in joyful fellowship with God. Religion isn't luxury; it isn't fancy work for idle rich, or for women who haven't any office routine. Religion isn't an accidental, beautiful spark, struck off as the hammers of history forge culture after culture upon the anvil of suffering and toil and hope. Religion is the lifeblood of the full self, the deepest necessity, the most imperious hunger of man. You and I are not full selves until we are in God's Presence and He is visibly in us, alive, energizing, glorying, making life miraculous. And no group and no culture is down upon the Rock until it knows its base in the Divine Order.

Every civilization that increases in secularity sows the seeds of its own self-destruction. And *meetings* become *secular.* We Quakers, immersed in our secular world — against which we should be living protests — we as individuals become *secular* in spirit, and God is a faint and shadowy form, whose reality rests upon hearsay. Are we *sacred individuals, holy men,* saintly souls ripened in His Presence, while unspoken purity and God-likeness pierce the shams of self-defense, whereby selfish, self-oriented men try to *excuse themselves to themselves?* If you and I are deep in the beauty and grace and comeliness of God, we all unconsciously strip bare all defense of other men against God. When we attack men's unbelief by words, then men defend themselves by words. But if God so lives in us that His imperative beauty and holiness shine through us upon others, God *penetrates* and pierces the mask, the sham, the hollowness, and men become exposed, naked, defenseless before God. And this self-confident, earth-contented culture needs to be stripped of its self-sufficiency and know itself in the light of *God's Life* and holiness. The secularity of Germany, with its denial of any deeper divine Reality than that of physical blood, the Aryan Blood, is only a modified and advanced stage of the same secularity that walks the streets of Philadelphia and Lansdowne, and comes into the meeting-house and sits in our benches. For when we, in actual practice, only know God by hearsay, and pay Him traditional deference, and when we rely chiefly upon our heads, upon our *economic* information, and upon our *political* shrewdness and our *social skill* to reconstruct the world, we are *secular*, and secularism is in our meeting-houses today.

Hasten unto God. For in Him is a holiness and beauty that answer to the deepest, deepest needs of us all as "Pearl-Merchants." I would plead for holy lives, such as arise out of fellowship with Him, lives not secular and boisterously worldly in backslapping camaraderie, in the effort to make religion appealing to the man who wants a little religion, but not *too much*. But lives that are like those of the disciples, of whom it was said, "They took notice of them, they that had been with Jesus." Such lives dart like an aurora borealis ray of light into the souls of others, and kindle them into flames of God in the heart. We need *spoken words* and printed words to awaken the world of pearl-merchants into a divine discontent. But the beginning of all messages is in living epistles, men who live in the *spirit* and

130

power and the Presence in which the Prophets and Apostles lived.

Hasten unto God. How can I say this, so that it isn't, in the slang phrase, "old stuff"? There is a depth of immersion in the Divine Life that in earlier years I never dreamed was possible. It has made the common, mild, gentle, halfhearted, conventional religiosity of many people seem so "*pitifully*" inadequate. George Fox knew this long ago. As a young man he was himself religious enough to be considered by his relatives to be good material for the ministry. But Fox himself had a hint that this degree of religious consecration was a scandal, a pittance, a travesty upon the deeps of religion for which he hungered, and of the resplendent glory of which, even in his discontent, he had a glimpse. He found that the preachers of his day *didn't know God.* They just read in books things *about* God.

Have you become disenchanted about the half-hearted religiosity you see about you? Has there gnawed around the margin of your conscience a feeling of disloyalty to a Heavenly Vision? Have you stilled that disquieting thought of complete and awful and irrevocable commitment to God beyond any degree that is commonly found? Have you said, "Other people take their religion wildly; I must be more balanced and use common sense"? Have you said, "If I followed out my God-hunger *absolutely*, people would think me crazy, and I'd do harm, by my fanaticism, to the cause of religion"? For shame! How much religious zeal is killed by so-called "common sense." The Society of Friends in recent years has been choking itself with common sense and sobriety. Better to run the possible risk of fanaticism by complete dedication to God than to run the certain risk of mediocrity by twenty percent dedication. Better to run the risk of being examined by a psychiatrist, as Fox was taken to a surgeon to have his excess blood drawn off, than to measure our lives by our mediocre fellows, and, achieving respectable security in religion, be satisfied if we strike the average. Concerning such, the Scriptures say, "They, measuring themselves, by themselves, are not wise." The Prophets come to the world and say, "*Thus saith the Lord.*" They don't say, "Thus saith the majority."

Hasten unto Him. Woo Him. Pursue Him. Yet, He, the Hound of Heaven, has been pursuing us through the years, baying ever on our track. It was *we* who needed to give assent to His Presence, not He who had to be attracted and come to us. And when He enters in and sups with us and we with Him, what unspeakable joy! At last we are Home. We are on the Rock. Life's end is in God, as its beginning and middle is in God. Such was Jesus' passion — the Father. Such is ours, if we Prodigals find we have wandered into a far country. Is God *your* passion? Do *you* long for Him and rejoice in Him and find life meaningful only to the degree you are in His Presence and He is in your life? Do you keep close to the Divine Center, the Inner principle counting all else as loss? For a depth of commitment such as mild men do not know, I speak in order that *you* may hear *Him* speak in you the same message. Out of such lives will the world be reborn, will the church be reborn. Hasten unto God, all you zealous pearl-merchants! There will you find rest for your souls, and power, and peace, and joy unspeakable and full of Glory.

Hasten unto God. I have spoken with deep feeling, for I am convinced this is the *deepest need* of all men. We Quakers have become earthy. We are more at home with humans than we are with God. We have men of burning social passion, but not so many that *burn for God,* who long for God, who go down deep into the Waters of His life, who call to us, "*O taste and see that the Lord is good.*" Social reformers we have now, men who are great in their contribution to social thinking to war, to peace, to economic injustice, to racial cooperation. But this epoch of history is weak in great prophets of the inner life, great voices who cry in the wilderness, "Prepare ye the way of the Lord within your hearts." Skill in social expressions of God is great; skill in communion with Him, agile obedience to the Inward Glory, is less common today. Plato could rightly say of this day as of his own, "Many are the thyrsus-bearers; few are the mystics." Strip monasticism; strip it of its retreat behind walls from much human need; strip it of its celibacy; and there is left, in Bernard of Clairvaux and Francis of Assisi, a God-hunger, and completeness of renunciation *of all else* in the world in comparison with the life that is hid with Christ in God.

Such a passion for God as leads men, for a time to leave father and mother and all the world, like an Eckhart, until *deep* relations with God have been found is hardly encouraged or even tolerated. We in this epoch of social-mindedness are in danger of a twenty-four-hour-day application of the cup-of-cold-water program. Bands of men and women and of serious youths who retreated temporarily for six months or a year from the world's needs, in order to deepen their fellowship with God, would be apt to be charged with misguided flight. Yet I am convinced that in the long run the world would be better off if there were an institution in our society for serious retreat into the depths, not of learned theological study, but of the practice of individual and group mysticism, for six months or a year. Such men and women, not with *social techniques*, but with God-motivations born out of deep immersion in the ocean of the Love of God. The specific tasks they would follow would be widely different. Their *skills* in techniques should be gotten in secular places. But down at the base of life, for all such people, would be a fellowship in a common Life which is the Light within every man who is kindled and enflamed by God.

Do not misunderstand me. There is a practice of the presence of God which is done on the run, in the busiest of days, in office, and schoolroom, and kitchen. Little prayers and communion; ejaculation of surrender and joy and exaltation; if it didn't sound silly to say it, little snugglings of the soul moving nearer to God. And most of our lives can be lived this way, as divine conversation of our soul with God, going on behind the scenes all the time. But then come crucial periods in life when the quest for God grows hot, when the hot breath of the Hound of Heaven is at our heels, when the heart cries out, "Give me the Presence or I die." And these are the times when we get beneath the conventional mildness of average religiosity, and find Him more fully, who is dearer than life itself. From these men and women will come the profound return to religion, i.e., the love of God and neighbor, which is so desperately needed.

ii

The First and Greatest commandment is to Love the Lord thy God with all thy heart and soul and mind and strength. This is that of which we have been speaking. But the second is like unto it: "Thou shalt love thy neighbor as thyself." Hasten into the world.

About the *techniques* of effective service in the world I shall have little to say. Our conferences and committee meetings are busy talking about techniques. But let us look at the *inner* side of life and work among men.

There are some of our fellow men we can love as we love ourselves. I don't mean the gracious, pleasant, cultivated acquaintances whose charming personalities we enjoy. There is a fellowship among those who have been baptized, deep under rolling waters of God's love, a fellowship too rich and precious to be described adequately. May I use two German words whose content and meaning are richer and thicker than our overworked word "Fellowship": *Gemeinschaft* and *Verbundenheit*. Among the early Apostles there was a *Gemeinschaft*, nay, deeper, there was a *Verbundenheit*, a condition of being knit together. The *Gemeinschaft*, this *Verbundenheit*, wasn't due to their common outer experiences. It was due to their common inner experience in God. They knew and loved one another because they all knew that they had found the same life-center. They had all gone deep into God, or God had gone down deep into them. In companionship with Jesus they had found His life-center and that center was in God. Such fellowships, such *Gemeinschaft*, nay *Verbundenheit*, as the Apostles had is a very real experience of group unity and amazing love. It is the stuff of the *Kingdom of God*. Early Friends knew this fellowship among themselves. They saw that, behind all the differences of education and age and social status, there was a Common Life-center, a blazing Light within, an ever-quickening Seed and Power, the Divine Pregnancy, this stirring of the life to new birth, this becoming larger with God within them— all who knew this and lived by it were in the Fellowship. You can love such neighbors as yourself even if you haven't known them in outer years as long as you have many an old friend.

It was a tragic day when the fellowship of the

early church groups faded out into church membership. And it was a tragic day when the fellowship of the early Children of the Light gave way to membership in a Society of Friends. From *Fellowship* to *Membership* is to cross a great and *tragic* divide. *Now*, when you meet a *member* of the Society of Friends, you don't know whether you can find *fellowship* with him at the deepest level within the Life-center in the Divine Seed, or whether you can only pass the time of day with him.

Oh, how one craves this fellowship! I have hungered for it *so* desperately in recent times. Now and then one finds a soul with whom one can have this deep *Gemeinschaft* grounded in membership in the Divine Life. But there are so many who are just *members* of the Society of Friends. Or else we have practiced living behind our own private curtains and never letting anyone in behind the screen. I know some very dear Quakers who, I am sure, know God intimately and love Him dearly, but who open only a crack of the door to others for this deeper fellowship.

How much of this deeper fellowship binds you together? Are you a group of *members*? Or do some of you form a nucleus of fellowship, while surrounding it is a lot of dead timber of conventional respectable Quakers? Such an inner nucleus may or may not be the inner group that carries the greater responsibility for the earthly, the meeting. I know a man in a nearby Quaker community who hasn't enough money and enough commanding personality to have much say about conduct of the meeting. But he knows the *Life*, and I find myself in deeper *Verbundenheit* with him than many more so-called influential members. On the other hand, our respectable members endure through all the burdens and heat of the day, of the meeting's problems more generally because they are grounded in the Divine Life.

But this deep fellowship is not an *accidental* fact in a living religious group. It is one of our most precious assets. We Americans are apt to be "rugged individualists," and not be extremely sensitive to this group *love* and fellowship. But, religious devotees make a *blessed* community; through the drawing of love one for another. And love for one another is rooted and grounded in the love of God, love toward God, love from God.

How can this *Gemeinschaft* be fostered? One thing needed, of course, is more Heaven-kindled, God-intoxicated souls. But some of these souls, I am sure, exist yet aren't able to make vivid this group love. Some of us are so reticent about the things of God, and never talk *with anybody*. Yet ought we not, for our own sakes, and for others? I think we ought to speak more freely about the deepest things of life. No, let's not get back to the days of evangelism when pious souls, all too loosely, buttonholed every neighbor and said, "Have you given your heart to Jesus?" But a tradition that it is a proper thing to talk about needs some development. But such talk has to be *real*, resting upon direct and growing knowledge of the upspringing, quickening Life of God within. Joy in the Lord, common rejoicing together, is normal and natural, *where the experience itself is real,* and there the sense of *being Members of one body arises.* Felt unity is very real. But articulated words, not about unity, but about God, bind us together in Christian Love. In this matrix of *Gemeinschaft,* or *Verbundenheit,* our souls grow and support one another and encourage one another and bear one another's burdens. And our individuality is no longer insulated from others, falsely, but we experience something of the unity-in-multiplicity which maintains individuals and groups as equally significant.

Another thing which may foster *Gemeinschaft* in a meeting like this is the laying hold upon the meeting for worship by each member, however insignificant, in deeper prayer and openness before God. What do you do in your hour of worship? Do you fidget and lay bets on which one on the facing benches will speak? Or is the facing seat performance so regularized that even the excitement of betting is taken away? Oh that we might break through the conventions of a formal, crusted-over meeting and face each other anew, and pour out our souls into that group worship, each one ready to speak or be silent as seems best. Have you who have never spoken, known times when you are disloyal to yourself and to God? Have you glossed over what was once a quickening impulse to give something to the meeting, but which you failed to do because of the unsteadiness of your knees? Have you a *right* to keep silent? "The lion hath roared; who can but tremble? The voice of the Lord hath spoken; who can but prophesy?" Amazing, amazing is the growth, the growth of unity and fellowship when one of our members shows growth in fidelity and sensitiveness.

Or, on the other hand, you who speak frequently in meeting, have you *always* asked yourself if you outran your leading? It is so easy to sit in front and think that silence has run long enough, and decide that something ought to be said to keep the meeting going. And thus one speaks with insufficient *inner exercise*. And having begun a talk on a *human* basis, not wholly on a God-prompted basis, we *decorate* it with sly bits of learnedness, which add nothing to its effectiveness, but give us as individuals a little private pride, for now others will know how learned we were. They'll think he's so full that he even lets such things slip in without knowing it! So we feed our pride before people. And sometimes all go away and say, "Wasn't that a lovely sermon?" For shame! Humility, deep, deep, searching humility that gives God all — out of such hearts speaks the Life that convinces. For we are to bring men away from all outer teachers, even from ourselves, and point them to the Inner Teacher, the Indwelling Christ, the Light, the Holy Seed, the Principle, the Center.

Little Children, love one another. My hair isn't as gray as was the hair of the centurion, John the beloved disciple, when they carried him into the assembly of the saints. But loving one another in the circle of those who know the open secret of the Glory of God is an easy thing. Hasten into this love of neighbor which is grounded in a common love of God. And make here a living cell in the body of the *Kingdom of God.* For the Kingdom of God consists in just this loving, blessed fellowship, the *Verbundenheit* among the "saints." Church members can hate one another. My membership is external, fellowship is divine and internal. If ye walk in the light as He is in the light, ye have fellowship one with another, and you love these, your neighbors, as yourselves. *Hasten unto these, your neighbors,* in the faith. But hasten unto them by *hastening unto God.* There is the root and the ground of that true fellowship and love that overcomes the world.

PART FOUR

Life in the Eternal Now

George Fox preached Christ present to teach His people himself. In these new additions to The Eternal Promise, *Thomas Kelly calls us to a life in that Reality: "Periods of quiet and meditation alone and in reverent groups should be a part of normal living for all who would go down into central silences which are to be found in the Heart of God."*

"Have You Ever Seen a Miracle?" is an address which will be new to many. Thomas Kelly's son, Richard, believes it was delivered to a group of United Church of Christ pastors at their annual retreat on the coast of Maine in 1940.

"Children of the Light" was written the weekend before Kelly's sudden death as a short declaration of his faith and devotion to the Light. It was to be read at the 1941 annual meeting of the Friends World Committee and the Fellowship Council. It was included in Thomas Kelly: A Biography *(Harper & Row, 1966).*

Have You Ever Seen a Miracle?

Have you ever seen a miracle? I have. Have you ever seen the water of ordinary human nature changed into the wine of divine creative living? I have. Have you ever seen men and women whose outer world was repellent, or tragic, or barren, or hopeless, yet who walked serene, triumphant, radiant, released, undismayed, living constructively, as if they were already in Eternity, and drew not their encouragement from time? I have. We all have. Such persons have meat to eat that the world knows not of. Their secret of life is not outside of them or around them, it is *within* them. In a rocky land, they have a well of water springing up within them unto Eternal Life. Are you such a miracle of radiant eternity lived in the midst of time? Am I such a miracle? Are we people whose lives cannot be explained by our environment, but only by saying, The Eternal Life and Love are breaking through into time, at these points?

Protestantism has been passing through an epoch of belief in *salvation by environment.* We have tried to pull the strings of economic and political and social factors which influence the outer condition of men. Much of our church effort, and much of our preaching has been this sort, in the past three decades. And this is very important, for the crushing load of environment can blight and blast many a potentially great soul. But, fundamentally, the world desperately needs people who are rooted deeper than their earthly environment, who have a stability so grounded, so deep, that environmental changes, so subject to the fickle winds of fortune, do not shake them. The time is here when we must get deeper than our external programs of church activities in time, and recover the sense of the Eternal Order and the Eternal Love as underlying the whole of time. And Protestants have been supposing that religious work consists in *doing things for God.* We have been the active ones, planning what we think are the logical consequences, in action, of the Gospel of Christ. And we have wanted God to be the passive receiver of our offerings, our services. But the time is come when we must go deeper, and learn that *God is the active one,* and learn that we are meant to be acted through. We must go down deeper, and discover, as a *way of living,* not as a belief, how to be *pliant,* how to *be worked through by God,* who has become a living internal dynamic deep within us. Then indeed we do become active, as never before; but it is an activity that is *God-initiated.* It seems strange to say it, but the dynamic center of religion is in *God,* not in us; the world is in His Hands, not in ours; the center of creative living is in God, deep down within us as a *lived fact,* not in our heroic Nietzschean efforts to live *for* Him. Over and around and within us all broods an active Love, or Life, a Presence, standing and knocking, in saint and sinner, regardless of environment. To that dynamic persuasive Love and Life we would yield our own little lives, and in bonded union with Him *be worked through*, in joyful submission.

How can we get down deep into this creative Center, where the Eternal Love enfolds us, vitally? What can we do to open the Springs of Eternity that are ever pressing at the base of our being, so that the amazing life of God Himself flows into us and organizes us into solid, triumphant, invincible, tranquil, energetic personalities, sweeps away our little fears and timidities, and rolls through us in new boldness, and flows out through us and waters a world with heavenly springs of power?

Let us be utterly honest tonight. I may appear to be speaking more to the ministers among you, but I really mean to speak to you all. Some of us have gotten so tangled with time, with committees, with service programs, with pushing about institutional machinery that we have lost something of the radiant glow of Eternity which we once saw dawning within us. The time was when God was very near, when heaven's joy was pressing upon us on every side, and the world seemed to lie at our feet, and at His feet. But now heaven's echo has grown distant, and we are weary, and somewhat disillusioned, and not wholly unspotted by the world. And the Sundays come crowding upon us, and we are spiritually dry. There isn't a sermon in the whole Bible, and we get our sermons out of books written by others who were on the flood-tide of the Spirit. We preach *beyond our own experience*, and then we despise ourselves inwardly for our hypocrisy in the pulpit. Sometimes we wish we could get out of the ministry, but we can't for we have a family to support, and we're too far along in life to change our profession.

We went into the ministry and into the Christian dedication, resolved to be men of God, holy men, men deep in the mysteries of God's love. We wanted to tell men simply about the breath-taking beauty of the Carpenter of Nazareth, and walk in simplicity, a good shepherd of sheep. But now we've grown *learned*, and a little proud of our learning, and anxious to keep up with the latest books. We've grown envious of the so-called bigger pulpits, and have slid over into professional ambition, and accepted the worldly standards of "getting ahead."

And our learned language, with which we try to hold the intelligentsia, whom we want most of all to reach, has become a hedge, a barrier, that keeps the little children and the simple folk away from us. We came to know the poorer, the squalid section of town chiefly through occasional visits for charitable purposes. But we have few *friends* among the poor and lowly. They are not people with whom we sit in the evening and chat, and visit eye to eye, and talk over, *in the spirit of give and take*, the meaning of life and death and suffering and heaven and God and love and joy and victory and surrender. Men and women don't come often to talk to us about the deep things of the Spirit, but about their family quarrels. Some time ago I asked a Protestant minister in Philadelphia if many mature souls came to him to talk about the wonders of the life with God which come only to those who are advanced in religious living, and he replied, "Not one single person." A few weeks ago I asked a Jewish rabbi the same question and his answer was even more devastating. He said, "If anyone comes to talk with me about religion I find he is psychopathic; only the religious cranks want to talk religion with me." Yet down beneath all this reticence, this surface preoccupation with external committees and activities, men and women and boys and girls are feeling the pressure of Eternity within them, for as the writer of Ecclesiastes says, "He hath set Thee forever in their hearts." When shall we become so alive with the Eternal Love that we break through into men's loneliness, and speak with one another in the deep silences of the heart?

O God of Abraham, God of Isaac, God of Jacob, God of the lowly Nazarene, restore unto us the joy of Thy presence and the glorious radiance of Thy beauty. Teach us, Thou inward Teacher of our Souls. Teach us to slough off our earthly, time-born pettiness, and walk in simplicity and lowly love all our days. Give us of Thy cosmic patience. Blind us to discouragement and to anxious fears, that we may put our hands trustingly in Thine, and become incarnate miracles of the Eternal Goodness breaking in upon a time-blinded world and a time-blinded church.

But not all is discouragement and dimness of vision. There comes time when Eternity is very near, when the curtains of heaven are lowered, and He who has shadowed over us all the years now leads us in green pastures and makes us to lie down beside the still waters. He restoreth our souls to their true Home in Him. Now we know at first hand, and immediately, what was the true situation all along, that the Eternal God is our refuge and underneath are the Everlasting Arms. Now we know what it is to dwell in the secret place of the Most High and to abide under the Shadow of the Almighty and to be bound into the bundle of life with God. And joy returns, an abandon of joy, deep-running and quiet, beyond any we have ever tasted before. And peace returns, a miracle of peace, experienced, and tasted. God's peace; our peace. Who can distinguish them? And serenity returns, a deeper serenity, a calm patience, an unhurried assurance, a resting, freed from anxieties, in Him. And power returns, and faith, a faith that really removes mountains, for now we see that God is active, dynamic, energizing, persuading. And our task is not to work for Him, but to learn for Him to *work through us and to join our sensitivity to His working*, already going on inside the lives of others. For wherever we go, there God has preceded us. To whomever we speak, God has first been speaking to him. And our task is to urge men to listen to their *inner Teacher*. Within all men the heavenly Educator is at work, tenderly, patiently, speaking inside of rich and poor, educated and ignorant, black and white. And the Church's task is first of all to call men to a listening life, a life of internal listening to the inner promptings that are already going on. We don't begin religion; *God begins it, knocking within*, in faint promptings, in inward appeals in the silences of our hearts. Young people hear Him, like the child Samuel in the quiet of the night. Our task is to *expect God* to be at work inside of young people, and to tell them to listen to their inner Teacher, the Divine Love, pressing upon the margins of their consciousness. Don't try to catch young people for the church by a jitterbug program of fevered activities. Help them to learn how to listen and *be quiet within themselves*. For the listening to the eternal involves a silence within us, a relaxed receptivity, a listening and an expectancy directed to a still small voice within. Periods of quiet and meditation alone and in reverent groups should be a part of normal living for all who would go down into central silences which are to be found in the Heart of God. And then steals in, again and again, a heavenly warmth, a sweet assurance, an invigorative solidity, a constructive integration of the will, a burning love for God, a falling of the scales from the eyes, so that one sees the world anew, simply, directly, as if through the eyes of the God of Love. I have no interest in silence as a *form*. But I know that devotion and dedication arise in the deep communings of the heart, in dwelling with a Silence in the center of our being. In periods of relaxed listening and expectancy the silence within us seems to merge with a creative silence within the heart of God and we hear Eternity's whispers, and we become miracles of Eternity breaking into Time. Live a *listening life*. Order your outward life so that nothing drowns out the listening. There is nothing more precious to preserve, to cultivate. If you think you haven't time for it, then ask if you are not pursuing *secondary values*.

I believe with all my heart in an empirical awareness of God. God is no rumor. God is no hearsay. God Himself shows His face in our inner life, in the secret places of our hearts. I have no great interest in the extremes of mystical ecstasies and in trances. I have no interest at all in emotional orgies and sentimental rhapsodies. But I do know that to common men and women like you and me, set in the midst of the wear and tear of life, come times of precious nearness, when the veil between time and Eternity grows thin and one feels the pulse-beat of the love of God. These are not times when one loses consciousness; the world of sight and touch do not fade away. One goes to work in the morning and returns in the evening, one meets one's friends and pays one's bills. But the Time-world where we usually live is not our only world. A second world seems to be about us, enclosing us and enclosing the whole of our Time-world and enwrapping all things into its loving embrace. In both worlds we live, at once; in the world of Time, but it is a new world of Time which is embraced and enfolded in the life of God. And about us and within us God quivers and quickens and strains and we go well-nigh mad with a calm and unutterable joy. Have you heard of the dance of Shiva that Hindu god who, standing in the center of the universe, dances, and out of Joy, creates this world? It is an amazing thing to find creativity in one's very heart!

.....I have felt
A Presence that disturbs me with the joy
Of elevated thoughts: a sense sublime
Of something far more deeply interfused,
Whose dwelling is the light of setting suns,
And the round ocean and the living air.
And the blue sky, and in the minds of man:
A motion and a spirit, that impels
All thinking things, all objects of all thoughts
And rolls through all things.

Such experiences are brief and passive. This splendor of God over all things lasts only a few minutes or a few hours or at best but a few days or weeks. It goes, as it comes, inexplicably, and beyond our control. No frantic prayers will prolong it; no frantic prayers will restore it; no frantic prayers will compel its arrival.

Here is a great pendular swing from depression

to elation, from deep spiritual dryness to unbounded spiritual exaltation. Is our religious life, our bondedness of soul with God an alternating, fluctuating bondedness, found only at one end of the oscillation and absent from the other? Is there a way of sinking down so deep into God's life that the great cyclic changes may come and go, and yet we are undismayed by the fading of the vision, but remain stable, firm, serene, grounded in Eternity? Is there a way of freeing our life from the fleeting quality of the moments of time, so that we walk serenely with God in the garden, whether in the heat or the cool of the day? I believe there is.

I fear that in trying to answer this question I must draw rather heavily upon my own inadequate experience, fostered and guided by some medieval and modern Roman Catholic books on the inner life. Modern Protestants have seen so much either to an extreme, external activism, or to intellectual problem-solving, or to orgiastic emotionalism, that there is little in devotional literature to guide and counsel maturing souls, in their inner life with God. In fact, most liberal Protestants seem to be afraid of deep immersion in matters of the interior life, fearful lest men lose their touch with this external world of time, the world of the hungry, the needy, the politically oppressed, the eco-nomically maladjusted. Some of you may be betraying this tendency by squirming inwardly, right now, saying, why doesn't the lecturer get on to practical problems, the problems of society today, and not bank on the inner life of the soul. But unless we grow rich in deep living of the soul in the Eternal Love we shall flatten out into the sands of intellectualism and humanitarianism. Until we grown rich and mature in God and *become persons* who have utterly died to themselves and are actually hid away with Christ in God, we shall have missed the inner wells of living water which spring up and make life miraculous, and the desert to blossom like the rose.

I have found that in the center of the religious life, on our part, is a continuous and quiet willing away of our lives, a willing of all that we are and all that comes to us, into the heart and the will of God, utter dedication of will, utter surrender of oneself into God's care, as a child trustingly surrenders to a father. Down beneath the fluctuating changes of heavenly elation and hellish discouragement we can carry on a well-nigh continuous prayer life of *submission*, "Father, into thy hands I commend my spirit." This internal prayer of submission of will we can carry in the very midst of our busiest days. There is a way of carrying on our mental life at two levels at once, but it only comes with practice. At one level of our mental life we can be talking with people, dealing with problems, carrying the burdens that our calling in time puts upon us. But beneath all this occupation with time we can be in prayerful relation with the Eternal Goodness, quietly, serenely, joyfully, surrendering our-selves and all that we are to Him. It is a deep interim directing of our wills, a willing away of our wills into the care of the divine will. Sometimes this deep subterranean willing of ourselves into the living care of the Eternal is worded in simple little phrases, repeated again and again. "Take all of me, take all of me, take all of me." This is probably best, at the beginning of this practice of a double mental life that has its mature birth in time and in Eternity. That is, in months or in years, words seem to be left behind, and the *attitude* of will of which the words were the expression, becomes more steady, without the aid of words. One must be perpetually reviewing the attitude, be perpetually *within* it, not like the woman who set a smile on her face then went away and left her face smiling. But this ever-sustained self-willing of the self into the arms of God — whence comes it? Do *we* begin it, and by gritted teeth and clenched fist continue it? No. No. It begins in those moments of blinding vision of the perfect holiness of God, in those moments when we find God takes the initiative and breaks in upon us and lets us sense a little of His amazing Splendor, and whispers to us that our old life of separate selfhood apart from Him is no life at all. And inwardly calls us home unto Himself. It begins, when, from the side of God, He breaks down the middle wall of partition between us and Himself. For God is at work, is active, is dynamic, is brooding over His universe, flowing creatively into existent things and in persuading, enveloping love, calling all love back in self-surrender and adoration unto Himself. It is an amazing thing to discover as a living experience, not as a set of believed words, that God is at the root of religious dedication; that God is active within you and me and all men initiating the return unto Himself, that God is actively shadowing over His world and powerfully persuading us to abandon the husks and straws and to return to the Father's house, where there is bread enough and to spare. What dedication of soul we engage in is *our* dedication. Yet seen still more deeply, what dedication of love we offer to God is prompted by the sheer beauty of His persuading, all-embracing Love. But we know increasingly that, whether elation or depression fills the upper levels of our conscious life, down deep within is a real bondedness of our life with God's life that is an essential situation, that does not come and go with fluctuating states of consciousness, that God is a persuading goodness moving us home into Himself.

Over a field of waving grain the sunshine and the shadow pursue one another in changing variety. Yet deep down in the soil the forces of life are pressing up into the roots and into the stalk and the wheat is nourished and the grain matures. The forces of life go in, unmoved by the sunshine or the shadow which pursue each other across the surface. Such is the soul that is down in the Center, down in the Eternal Life, matured and ripened in the way of God's dealing with Love. In poised, serene assurance it welcomes the sunshine of divine favors in the soul, yet does not clamor for their continuance. In poised serene assurance it passes into the dry season of the spirit where God's face seems outwardly to be withdrawn, yet feels no anxiety. For God disciplines our souls and teaches us. Sometimes He refreshes us with each season's refreshments as to make our hearts well nigh burst with joy. And sometimes He withholds His face from us outwardly like the shadow across the grain. Our first reaction when we are spiritually babes is to clamor for the sunshine and grieve when it is gone. We say God has forsaken us. We have lost faith. We have displeased God. We long "to recapture that first rapture" and we clamor and struggle and grieve and think we have been unfaithful or neglectful of God. But such clinging to seasons of glory is a sign that we shall cling to self-love, self-will, self-pride, self-orientation. We want the vivid sense of God's Presence. O, that we may enjoy Him. It is *we* who are to be pleased and God is expected to supply us with spiritual pleasure. And as long as we want God for the sake of the good things He can give us, even the good things of the joy of His Presence, we are oriented around ourselves, not around Him. And as long as we rebel against seasons of spiritual dryness because they are *faithful to us*, we do not yet love God for His own dear sake, but chiefly for what He can give us, but sometimes withholds from us. Self-surrender is by no means complete when we demand that God furnish us with the pleasures of Paradise continually. We may even be perilously near to the danger of *spiritual sensuality*.

No, self-surrender becomes complete when we accept *all* God's dealings with our souls as a gift of

His grace and as token of His love. Does He show His face and make us to sit down in heavenly places in Christ Jesus? Than thank Him and be quietly but unboundedly grateful for His favor. Does He withdraw His inner consolation? Then thank Him for the discipline He thus lays upon us, that we may be weaned away from dependence upon the highs and lows of mental changes and learn *solely to cling to Him*, and learn to love Him purely for His own sake, and not for His gifts.

For spiritual maturity is not tested by the frequency of our mystical moments of exaltation, but by the glad and calm serenity of will in Him which is ours when barrenness and dryness come upon us. The Dark Night of the soul is an advanced course in the curriculum of the school of the Holy Spirit. And happy is he who has fulfilled the earlier prerequisites to whom is now entrusted this discipline of pain.

But it is not alone that we are freed from the changing sunshine and shadow of spiritual dryness and spiritual elevation, as we seek down, deep, below both, into quiet, resting of will in the Eternal Goodness. We reach a wholly new evaluation of outward things, a new indifference to personal fortunes or to fame as obscurity sets in. I like to call this the *royal blindness*. We grow blind to the petty valuations of the world. We grow blind to the petty eminences we have sought. We grow blind to the obscurity which is our lot, and, in no resentment, joyfully live in Eternity *just where we are*. Oh, we've known intellectually all these things for years, and have probably preached them from our pulpits. But there is an experience of finding all things levelled in the God-blinded eye which is utterly different from an intellectual belief in the unimportance of fame and obscurity. With what pity we now look upon men and women whose whole life and love seem to be set upon puny perishing tinsel! And with what shame we look upon our own wasted years of yearning to be somebody. For now we see these things as what they are: round-about ways of pleasing our *own little selves*, of freeing our own little selves from mental disquiet. O, we persuaded ourselves that we wanted a bigger church, a more prominent church, so we could have a bigger field of service, and help bring in the Kingdom more effectively. But now we know it was because we like the flattery of having people whisper behind our backs as we go by, "There goes so-and-so, he's quite an important man." And we've chafed in our tiny unnoticed niches because of wounded self-pride, because secretly we believed we were a bigger person than we got credit for being. Self-love, self-pride, self-seeking, self-inflation that would cover up its own poverty by accumulating an array of glittering earth garments of doctor's degrees and titles and honors and successes! But, O how sinuous and subtle is self-pride. The enemy of complete dedication! We preach clever sermons, and quote learned authors and hope men will notice how well-read we are. Do you recall that wise minister to whom a doting parishioner said, "O, Doctor Jones, that was a wonderful sermon you preached this morning." "Yes," replied the minister, "the Devil whispered that same thing to me, just as I was sitting down." Recall the words of St. Paul, "We preach not ourselves but Christ Jesus, and Him crucified, and ourselves your servants for Jesus' sake."

But the royal blindedness levels all this, to the degree that all our self is willed into the life and love of God, in utmost dedication. We can look past the riches of the rich man, right through the imposing front of artificial importance, and as Jesus did with the rich young man, love him for what he is, and yearn over him as a human, God-hungry, perhaps earth-blinded soul; yearn that he may be stricken with the royal blindedness of Eternity so that he too sees all men as levelled and himself as a humble child of God, and his wealth as a barrier or an opportunity or a trust. We can look past the learning of the learned, and pray that they be loosed from pride in their learning and be humbled and born again as little children. For of such, not of professors, is the Kingdom of Heaven.

And, O hardest test of all put upon the royal blindedness, we can meet the poor and the lowly in such utter sincerity of friendship and concern that some of them at least will find where the roots of our lives go down, and will look upon us with level eye and say, "I too am hungry for God. I too have seen some of His glory." But what terrible sincerity it takes. Only the simple directness of Jesus and of Francis of Assisi can do it. I am distressed that I know so many *nice* people, and have so few real personal friends among the Negroes and the roustabouts and the hopelessly submerged men and women. We try to pull the strings of political and social changes so as to better their broad environment. And all this is important. But Christ is not born in us until we see them as persons, and visit as friends in their homes, and know their hopes and anxieties, the fears of old age, and of sickness, the deep, deep God-hunger that is planted in them as in us all. Then Christ walks on the streets again. When, being at home among the great and comfortable, we count these starched respectabilities as things not to be grasped, but humble ourselves and take on ourselves the fashion of humble men, and being made humble as the humblest man by the levelling blindness of love, we become obedient, even unto death. Yea, if it be His will, the death of a cross.

But the royal blindness leads us also into stupendous ventures of faith. It set Paul and Barnabas, two lonely men, backed only by the good will of the Antioch Church, to conquer the Mediterranean world for Christ. All rational calculations were against them. But blinded by Eternity within them, they saw no unconquerable obstacle in time. It set John Woolman, a humble tailor of New Jersey, to root out Negro slavery in this country. An absurd undertaking in 1750! But in 1800 every single slave owned by Quakers in Pennsylvania and New Jersey had been set free voluntarily, and the movement was rolling which issued in Abraham Lincoln and the Emancipation. Do you see *war* as a giant, iniquitous, futile, unChristian system? Then hurl yourself against it, in full blindness to the seeming impossibility of the task. For if God be for us, who can be against us? Does profit-seeking as the main stem of business strike you as the root of great evils? There are no impossibles to those who, in supreme dedication, are rooted deep in the Eternal Love. One shall overcome a thousand and two shall put ten thousand to flight, and the gates of hell shall not prevail against them. These are high words, but not lightly spoken. For creative, recreative, world-overturning living is possible when we as individuals and when the church as a fellowship become God-possessed channels through which the creative Love flows into the world of men. Serene, unhurried, undismayed, miraculous lives can be lived by you and by me, if we continuously will away the last vestige of claim upon ourselves and become wholly God-enthralled.

Children of the Light

The Light for which the world longs is already shining. It is shining into the darkness, but the darkness does not apprehend it. It is shining into the darkness, but the darkness is not overcoming it. It is shining in many a soul and already the new order has begun within the kingdom of the heart. It is shining in many a small group and creating a heavenly-earthly fellowship of Children of the Light. It will always shine and lead many into the world of need, that they may bear it up into the heart of God.

With trembling awe at the wonder which is ever wrought within us, we must humbly bear the message of the Light. Many see it from afar and long for it with all their being. Amidst all the darkness of this time the day star can arise in astounding power and overcome the darkness within and without.

It is given to us to be message-bearers of the day that can dawn in apostolic power if we be wholly committed to the Light. Radiant in that radiance, we may confidently expect the kindling of the Light in all men until all men's footsteps are lighted by that Light, which is within them.

Our fellowship groups are small, but they can

be glorious colonies of heaven, cities set on a hill. It is a great message which is given to us — good news indeed — that the Light overcomes the darkness. But to give the message we must also be the message!

Index

This index covers three of Thomas Kelly's works: *The Eternal Promise* (EP), *A Testament of Devotion* (TD), and *The Reality of the Spiritual World* (RSW). Though it is hardly exhaustive, the index should help readers find various passages in which Kelly discusses similar themes.

DATE DUE

HIGHSMITH   #LO-45220